For mum and dad . . .

who instilled in me a love of learning and a deep sense of curiosity.

Trust Yourself:

How empowered decision-making will help you resolve your family law matter

The material in this book is provided for information purposes only. The reader should consult with his or her personal legal, financial and other advisors before utilising the information contained in this book. The author and the publisher assume no responsibility for any damages or losses incurred during or as a result of following this information.

There are many legal principles included in this book which the author has explained in her own way. If required, specific references can be provided on request.

All names referred to in this book have been changed to protect the identity of the individual.

INDEPENDENT INK

First published 2018 by Independent Ink
This second edition published 2023
PO Box 1638, Carindale
Queensland 4152 Australia

Cover design by Jo Hunt and updated by Catucci Design
Back cover photography by Jason Malouin
Illustrations and checklists by Boldly Creative
Typeset in 11/17 pt Bembo by Post Pre-press Group, Brisbane

Cataloguing-in-Publication data is available from the National Library of Australia

ISBN 978-0-6458852-1-7 (pbk)
ISBN 978-0-6458852-0-0 (epub)

contents

Prologue

If you were offered the opportunity to determine your family law outcome by being equipped with a deep understanding of your facts, the law, the system, the reality and your goals, would you take it? A process that empowered you to make key decisions, resolve your family law matter and get on with your life surely is appealing.

I call this **empowered decision-making** – that is, having knowledge about the law, the system, your matter, the reality and how those variables align with your goals, all of which will give you the power to make decisions that accord with the outcomes you are trying to achieve.

I love being a lawyer. I love assisting people and helping them work towards a solution to whatever their legal problem might be. I love educating my clients about the law, explaining how it applies to them and imparting knowledge so they are better informed about their legal issue (and ideally won't fall into the same issue again, or be better informed if they do).

I'm not sure where my thirst for knowledge about the law began. In my formal schooling I wasn't academic, and I did only enough work to get through. It took me several years to work out what career I wanted to have. I muddled my way through parts of an information technology degree, hospitality diplomas and teaching. In 1998 I stumbled into my law degree – not due to any strong sense of justice or to right wrongs, but because a friend was studying law and I thought, *That sounds interesting*. Right up to the conclusion of my law degree I maintained that I was studying out of interest's sake only. I chose subjects that were interesting to me. It was only in my last semester of study that I decided to pursue a career in the law – I thought, *Well, I've done all this study – might as well do something with it!*

I completed my practical training and was lucky enough to be placed in a general practice law firm with a focus on family law, which needed new lawyers. I was offered a job on day two. Suddenly there I was – a lawyer in training at age 27. It's 18 years now since I started that job, in the same law practice I now own. I moved from trainee lawyer to lawyer, to partner, to owner. To have my contribution to the law practice recognised in this way has provided me with a sense of achievement and purpose.

Perhaps there was something greater at work that led me to this path. Perhaps by heading along to a law lecture one day I was subconsciously taking a step to work out what I wanted to do, and got hooked. Whatever the reasoning behind it, I *am* now hooked, and there is nothing more satisfying than bringing about a positive outcome for a client I believe in, whether it be restoring access to the father falsely accused of abusing his daughter, or providing the mother in a family violence situation with a sense of reassurance and calm.

Since beginning work as a lawyer, I've found my thirst for knowledge and learning has sparked like never before. The more I work as a lawyer the more I want to continue to refine my skills every day, learn about different aspects of the law and keep up to date with the latest developments in family law. The spark has seen me through the completion of a Master of Laws, and thereafter a Master of Applied Law (Family Law).

After knowledge, the second most influential component of my everyday life is education. I can often be heard saying to clients, staff, friends and family, *Every day is a school day.* By this, I mean we all have regular learning experiences. I believe there is great power in learning about things and acquiring knowledge. I'm passionate about imparting knowledge to clients, other lawyers and students. Whether it is providing clients with detailed advice so that they are fully informed in making decisions about their matter, or speaking with students at the local secondary school about topics they are studying or options they might consider for when they graduate, the ability to share my knowledge gives me great joy.

So I wanted to write this book and share the knowledge about family law that I have with you – whether you have a current legal issue, or may not know that you have one, or just need a little information to get started on your legal journey.

This is the second edition of *Trust Yourself*, originally published in 2018 and revised and updated in 2023 to let you know about significant changes to our Family Court system which came into effect in 2021. I hope you find this information useful.

Elizabeth

Introduction

The law touches every person throughout their days, weeks and lives without many people really being aware or having reason to question it. From the transaction to purchase a new car (signing a contract) to buying a new surfboard (sale of goods), moving into a new property (contract or tenancy agreement) or having a lovely meal out (food and licensing requirements), daily life goes on without much need to think about these legal transactions.

The law is generally only considered when things go wrong, when a dispute occurs or when you start planning your future. By this time you might find it is too late, you are in more trouble than you thought or things are more messy or out of order than they need to be. Generally though, most people get by without having to consider the law or talk to a lawyer.

If you are separating from your spouse, it is more likely that you will need to consider the family law and its impact on your separation, whether this involves your property settlement or the arrangements for your children. There are good reasons, at the very least, to have a preliminary discussion with a family lawyer to make sure you are on track, even if you ultimately work everything out.

To give a sense of the number of families who access the family law system annually, in the 2021–22 year, approximately 109,000 applications were lodged with the Federal Circuit and Family Court of Australia, and the Family Court of Western Australia (the two courts that deal with family law matters) combined.

Across Australia, just under half of the applications lodged are Divorce Applications (about 52,000). Just under 16,000 are new applications filed seeking parenting orders, property orders or both. About 19,000 applications are for Consent Orders, where an agreement is reached without the need to file a contested application. The balance of applications are those filed within proceedings or other applications.

When considering how long a matter takes to conclude, the average length of time for a matter to move through the court system is increasing. In Western Australia, the timeframe has risen from 91 weeks in 2017 to 140 weeks in 2022. In the Federal Circuit and Family Court of Australia, the time has increased from around 16 months in the 2019–20 year to 19 months in the 2021–22 year. Both Courts report the increasing complexity of matters as a primary reason for the increase in time.

In practice we have seen that historically, the average family law matter going to trial will take between 2 and 4 years. Parties can wait 12–18 months for a final hearing from the time the court deems that the matter is ready for a final hearing.

These delays were a significant reason behind the restructure of the Court system and the introduction of the new Case Management Pathway in September 2021. The intention of the new pathway is to see matters through the Court system within 12 months, with specific rules regarding appearances, the number of interim hearings, the need for mediation and an early trial. Anecdotal evidence suggests that matters are moving through quickly. There is a push within the Court system to clear the older pre-merge 'legacy' matters to improve the overall functioning of the Court and, importantly, for litigants to move through the system as quickly as possible.

Returning then to the question I posed at the beginning:

If you were offered the opportunity to determine your family law outcome by having a deep understanding of your facts, the law, the system, the reality and your goals, would you take it?

Early in my career, I recognised that there is value in people and their families being armed with information; people so often go through life without protecting themselves, their dignity, their future and their relationships. Time and time again I have experienced clients who have a personal legal issue as being reactive and lacking the knowledge to move forward. They are often looking for a speedy resolution of their matter, at fair cost and as an end to their distress. I have found that through encouraging them to focus on their goals, gain knowledge about their legal matter and implement a well-thought-out strategy, clients can become informed, empowered and focused. They know their end game and ultimately achieve peace of mind in the awareness that their issue is resolved.

There are so many variables within the family law system – the personalities at play, the court, the judge, the outcome generally. The New South Wales Court of Appeal has said in *Studer v Boettcher* [2000] NSWCA 263, per Fitzgerald JA, at para 63:

it is often impossible to predict the outcome of litigation with a high degree of confidence. Disagreements on the law occur even in the High Court. An apparently strong case can be lost if the evidence is not accepted, and it is often difficult to forecast how a witness will act in the witness-box. Many steps in the curial process involve value judgments, discretionary decisions and other subjective determinations which are inherently unpredictable. Even well-organised, efficient courts cannot routinely produce quick decisions, and appeals further delay finality. Factors personal to a client and any inequality between the client and other parties to the dispute are also potentially material. Litigation is highly stressful for most people and notoriously expensive. An obligation on a litigant to pay the costs of another party in addition to his or her own costs can be financially ruinous. Further, time spent by parties and witnesses in connection with litigation cannot be devoted to other, productive activities. Consideration of a range of competing factors such as these can reasonably lead rational people to different conclusions concerning the best course to follow.

So why would you take on those odds? It seems madness to willingly walk head-on into a system so fraught with unpredictability. Appreciating that some matters will ultimately end up before a court given the personalities at play or the technical legal issue to be resolved, given the choice any family lawyer would advise you to avoid the court system at all costs.

If you are contemplating separation or a change in your relationship circumstances, this book is for you. Regardless of where you live in Australia, this book will provide you with information about family law. While Western Australia has a separate family law system to the rest of Australia, the concepts and principles are the same. The references to the law and court will be different; however, the system and realities mentioned throughout this book apply wherever you live.

Note that this book is written as an information guide only. It should not be read as advice specific to your personal circumstances. You should always consult with a family lawyer to obtain legal advice about your individual circumstances.

In this book you will find information about the family law system, the law as it relates to families, and *information* (which is not the same as *advice*) about how to stay out of the family law court or move through the courts with ease. This book provides you with *information* about how to be empowered to best determine your family law outcome and move on with your life as soon as possible.

In **Chapter 1** you will find a brief overview of the family law system and the *Family Law Act*. You will also find information about the different variables that can influence your family law matter.

Chapter 2 looks at the types of relationships covered by family law in Australia, and in particular provides you with important information about what it means to be in a de facto relationship.

In **Chapter 3** you will find information about separation, property matters, parenting matters and spouse maintenance. There is information about the current family law that would be applied to your family law matter.

Chapter 4 is devoted to domestic and family violence, and the importance of getting advice in this critical and specialised area.

In **Chapter 5** you will find information about ending your relationship, whether that means applying for a divorce if you are married, or formally ending your de facto relationship.

Chapter 6 sets out the steps involved in going to court. This chapter looks at what is involved in starting proceedings and the processes you will come across as you progress through the court system.

Chapter 7 sets out the practical steps you can take to resolve your matter by alternative means – such as attending mediation, arbitration and other ways to avoid the court system – or get you out of the court system sooner. This chapter also covers the documents you can prepare to finalise your property or parenting settlement.

In **Chapter 8** you will find information about choosing the right family lawyer and preparing for your first consultation.

Chapter 9 is all about empowered decision-making, and reveals my personal process to assist you in resolving your family law matter in an empowered way.

In **Chapter 10** you will find ground rules for an amicable settlement as well as tips and advice about looking after your mental health and financial needs.

In the conclusion, I pull all of the critical information together for you.

Finally, in the **Resources** section at the end of this book, you will find key information and contact details for organisations that can assist you. You will also find key checklists that you can review and use when preparing for your visit to your family lawyer. These are also available online – the details of where you can find them are also in this section.

It is on that basis that I commend this book to you. While it is important that you do get legal advice about your own individual matter, what you will find in this book is information in a format you can understand to equip you to move forward with finding a solution to your legal issue. I hope you find empowerment in reading and learning from it, as much as I have from writing it.

Chapter 1:

Family law and the *Family Law Act*

Family law in Australia has developed over time, with early family law being adopted from the United Kingdom. Since 1975 Australia has had one system of family law that applies to all states and territories – aside from Western Australia, which elected not to join the commonwealth system at the time. While the law and processes are in essence the same, Western Australia has retained its own rules and court system. If you are in Western Australia, this book will provide you with a general understanding of family law in Australia; however, you should consult a local lawyer.

A BRIEF HISTORY OF THE DEVELOPMENT OF FAMILY LAW IN AUSTRALIA

Historically, the laws relating to family law focused on the status of women at the time of their marriage. The woman was in essence absorbed into the status of the man such that she did not have her own separate and distinct legal personality. In the 1760s, Sir William Blackstone's *Commentaries on the Laws of England* contemplated that 'the very being or existence of the woman is suspended during the marriage, or at least is incorporated or consolidated into that of the husband: under whose wing, protection and cover she performs everything'.

As time progressed and women's rights strengthened, the law evolved, with reform eventually occurring through the English *Matrimonial Causes Act 1857*, adopted across Australian colonies in due course. While divorce became more attainable, it still required a fault-based reason to institute proceedings, with acts of the husband needing to be particularly bad (physical acts of assault or cruelty) versus simply proving that the wife had been adulterous. From 1870, women gained the right to own property, separate from the assets of their husbands.

At the same time, the welfare of children was becoming the primary concern in determining parenting matters. Particularly for young children, it was at that time considered that children should stay with their mothers.

The *Family Law Act 1975* significantly departed from the historical laws of England and put in place a no-fault system of separation. The early versions of the Act reflected the social norms of the nuclear family at the time, with roles of the father as breadwinner and the mother as homemaker. The current version of the *Family Law Act*, by contrast, starts with the presumption that parents have an equal role of parenting their children.

Family law has adapted and changed to respond to social norms. The 1990s saw a focus on mothers primarily caring for their children. The 2006 amendments saw a push for mothers and fathers to be recognised equally in roles of caring for their children. Mothers and fathers may both work or not work. There are children and stepchildren; there are first, second and third partners. Grandparents care for children where their parents cannot. Stepparents care for stepchildren even after separation. While the traditional or nuclear family may have been the norm in the 1950s and 1960s, and still exists today, there are more and more variations on what it means to be a family in modern-day Australia.

As this book goes to print there is another review of the *Family Law Act* underway. The Attorney-General and various stakeholders are considering whether the provisions relating to parenting orders should be refined with the overall aim of making the determination of parenting arrangements simpler for separating parents and the courts. (You can read more about some of these proposed changes in **Chapter 3**.)

WHAT IS FAMILY LAW?

Family law is the body of law that sets out the steps to be taken and the principles that apply when making decisions for separated parties, whether set down in the *Family Law Act* (and other Acts) or in cases that have been decided since 1975. This includes whether parties can apply for a divorce to formally end their marriage, how their property should be divided, and how the children should spend time with each of their parents.

The practice of family law is the application of legislation (*Family Law Act*) and legal principles developed in cases to the facts and circumstances of a matter involving separated parties, their property and their children. In applying family law expertise, a legal advisor must be able to critically analyse the circumstances of each matter and advise on strategies and solutions to solve the problems presented to them by a client.

Family law can be seen as the intersection of many different areas of law. A family lawyer, in advising on various issues, may be confronted with legal issues that arise from other areas including domestic violence, wills and estate planning, tax, property and corporate structures – just to name a few.

VARIABLES IN FAMILY LAW MATTERS

For a person going through separation, there are often great issues at stake requiring more than just a positive attitude to get through the process. For example, your living arrangements are likely to change. The time you spend with your children is likely to be affected in some way. The property and wealth that you have acquired may be halved or divided into some other share.

There are other variables that will impact the outcome for you, and they will be different to those of the person sitting next to you on the train going to work, who might be going through what seems to be the very same family law matter. The following variables will be at play in any family law matter, no matter the circumstances:

- the law;
- the system;
- and your story/facts.

Let's explore those variables a little further.

The law

The law is complicated. As I've said, there is no one-size-fits-all answer for every matter. The law has developed over years and years. As I mentioned earlier in this chapter, the *Family Law Act* commenced in 1975 as legislation setting out the framework to be applied in family law matters. There is case law stemming from cases decided over decades of interpreting the framework and providing guidance to determine matters. There are different judges in different locations – from the court next door to the next city and other regional areas – all with their own individual interpretation of the law.

As you'll see in the chapters that follow, which set out a summary of the law as it relates to property and parenting matters, there are so many different variables within the law that might apply to your story.

The system

The family law system is not perfect, as any family lawyer will tell you. Politicians will from time to time try to reinvent the wheel by tweaking various aspects of the system or promising a full overhaul – at the time of writing, there is yet another review of the *Family Law Act* being undertaken. Regardless, the system is what it is. It's clunky. It doesn't suit every matter. This is one good reason why you might choose to work to resolve your matter outside of court.

Your story/facts

A family matter becomes a family law matter when parties separate and guidance is required to assist them in working out the best arrangements for their children and how to distribute their property. Each family law matter is unique to the individual involved. Family lawyers are often asked, 'My friend Sally went through the exact same scenario and her outcome was x – will my outcome be the same?' The answer is no. Unless the client's life is identical to Sally's in every single way – when they were born, who they married, when they married, what property they had and now have – there are factors that will differ in every matter. It is for this reason that your individual story is a variable that must be taken into account.

Say you had three neighbouring families living in the same street. It is highly unlikely that they would all have the same lives. Let's consider these scenarios:

James and Kate at house 1 are in a de facto relationship. They aren't planning on getting married. They have two children together, and James has a daughter from a previous relationship. They rent their home and do not own any other properties. They also have some superannuation.

Sharon and Samantha live in house 2. They have three investment properties as well as the home that they live in. They have a daughter and have just decided to get married, having lived together for eight years.

Marcello and Heather live in house 3, and have been married for 30 years. They have two children who are now independent adults. Heather has started to fear for her safety as Marcello drinks a lot more now that they have retired and has become physically violent towards her.

It is unlikely that you will find identical families in any given neighbourhood. All three of these families have different needs that would have to be considered if they were to separate. James and Kate might focus their efforts on their parenting arrangements, and Kate would need to consider whether she wants to maintain a relationship with James's daughter. Sharon and Samantha would need to consider formally applying for a divorce if they marry in the future and then separate, along with considering their property settlement and parenting matter. Heather would need advice about domestic and family violence, and might need assistance getting into a refuge. She and Marcello would also need to consider a property settlement.

Another aspect to consider before moving on is, as it is often said, that there are three sides to every story: one side, the other side and the truth, which lies somewhere in the middle. This isn't a criticism of anyone's representation of their own story. It certainly isn't an indication that no clients are truthful. The reality is that our experiences are coloured by our own perceptions. We all experience life through our own thoughts, feelings and senses, which affect how we see the world. It is likely, therefore, that how you see the world will be different to how the person sitting next to you on that train does.

Now that you have a picture of the family law system as a whole and you've seen the variables that can impact the outcome of your family law matter, we can move on to the following chapters to look at the areas most commonly dealt with in family law matters: parenting arrangements, property settlement, child support and spouse mainte-nance. First, though, we'll investigate different forms of relationship as understood in family law.

Chapter 2:

Defining marriages and de facto relationships

WHAT RELATIONSHIPS ARE COVERED BY FAMILY LAW

The Australian *Family Law Act* sets out the law for people who are married and people who are in a de facto relationship. From 2018, this includes both heterosexual and same-sex marriages, as well as de facto relationships.

Marriage

Marriage is defined in the *Marriage Act 1961* as the union of two people to the exclusion of all others, voluntarily entered into for life.

When two people get married it is easy to evidence the legal side of their relationship. They will have had a ceremony – either religious or with a civil celebrant – and will have a certificate of marriage that confirms the date on which and the place where they were married.

De facto relationships

For de facto relationships it isn't so clear. While you can register your relationship by lodging a form with the Registry of Births, Deaths and Marriages in your state, you don't need to, so it will ultimately come down to an agreement about when you started living together.

We've been together six months, so we are in a de facto relationship, right?
So you've been dating for a little while now and have taken the plunge to move in together. Your six-month anniversary of cohabiting ticks over. Your friends or associates say, 'Six months – he/she can take half your property now ...' Right? No – not quite.

It's a common misconception that if you have lived together with someone for six months that your relationship status is elevated to a point where one spouse might be able to claim property of their partner. While living together is one factor that is taken into account, the law is a little more complex than that.

What does the law say?

A de facto relationship exists where:

- two people have been living together on a genuine domestic basis for a period of two years; or
- two people have been living together on a genuine domestic basis for less than two years; however, they have a child together or have purchased property together.

The factors set out in the *Family Law Act* (section 4AA) that are taken into account when considering whether two persons have been living together as a couple on a genuine domestic basis are:

- the duration of the relationship;
- the nature and extent of their common residence;
- whether a sexual relationship exists;
- the degree of financial dependence or interdependence, and any arrangements for financial support, between them;
- the ownership, use and acquisition of their property;
- the degree of mutual commitment to a shared life;
- whether the relationship is or was registered under a prescribed law of a state or territory as a prescribed kind of relationship;
- the care and support of children;
- the reputation and public aspects of the relationship.

Commonly from a separation perspective, a key issue can be whether a de facto relationship exists at law.

Take Suzanne, for example. Suzanne and Scott have lived in an on-again, off-again relationship for over five years. They met and started going out together in about 2012. They live together for periods at Scott's parents' home, they live separately at other times. They do not have any children. They have a sexual relationship. They present as a couple to their friends and family. Some years into their relationship they purchase a property together. They share equally in payments for mortgage. Scott pays for the rates and utilities. About six months after they purchased this property, Suzanne and Scott separate their living arrangements. They continue to see each other on and off, and maintain their sexual relationship. About a year after the purchase of the property Suzanne ends the relationship.

It is more than likely that a de facto relationship exists in these circumstances. Suzanne and Scott own property together, they present as a couple to their family and friends, and they have lived with each other from time to time.

Whether a relationship exists at all is often argued about in matters with short relationships, particularly where one party to the relationship has significant assets in their own name and the existence of a de facto relationship may mean that the other party possibly has a claim to those assets.

If it is difficult to establish on evidence that a relationship existed as set out above, the person who is trying to assert a relationship has little or no options under the *Family Law Act*.

What if you are in a relationship with more than one person?

Meet Jasmine. Jasmine was in a long-term relationship with George for nine years. George says the relationship was only for three years. Jasmine had a property in her name at the beginning of the relationship. George also had a property in his name. During the relationship,

George acquired two further properties in his own name. Jasmine and George lived together in George's property. They presented to their family and friends as a couple. They attended family gatherings, weddings and funerals as a couple. Jasmine was able to produce invitations addressed to both of them throughout their relationship.

While they didn't have any children, Jasmine and George both made contributions to the relationship. Jasmine managed the accounts and at times paid bills for George on his behalf. Jasmine assisted in finding the properties that George purchased.

Upon separation, George claimed that they did not have a de facto relationship. The basis of this claim was that they had no joint property and that George had been maintaining a relationship with another woman for the last three years. George and this other woman did not live together, though, because she was still married to another man.

Now this is quite a complex matter which all comes down to the evidence that both parties can produce about their relationship. The key point here, however, is that just because George was in a relationship with another person at the same time as his relationship with Jasmine, doesn't mean that the de facto relationship between Jasmine and George didn't exist.

Many cases seeking a property settlement involving a de facto relationship also seek a declaration that the relationship existed at law, particularly where it is disputed by one party or ended very close to the two-year period.

Registering a de facto relationship

You can find information about how to register your de facto relationship by contacting the Registry of Births, Deaths and Marriages in your state. This is one aspect of family law that is still managed by the individual states.

The weblinks to the registries are found in the **Resources** section of this book.

Now that we are clear on the types of relationships that are covered by family law, we will move on to separation and the law that is applied to property and parenting matters.

Chapter 3:

Separation

The circumstances on separation for each couple are unique. While there are some aspects that could be seen to apply to lots of couples, it is not possible to cover each and every scenario in this book. On a day-to-day basis in our law practice, we advise clients about a number of family law issues. Generally, though, I can group four categories of clients who come in for advice:

- Those clients who have just separated and are seeking guidance about where to go from here. For these clients, often the reality of their separation is just sinking in.
- Clients who have been separated for a little while, where things have been going along okay. These clients have been taking their time to process their separation, or something has happened to cause them to seek advice.
- Clients who have separated, recently or some time ago, who have reached agreement and need assistance to document their agreement in order to finalise their matter.
- Clients who are not yet separated, seeking preliminary advice about separation generally. When considering ending a relationship, some clients recognise the need for advice prior to making such a significant and life-changing decision.

Our clients see us for all types of family law matters covered in this book – property and parenting, just property, just parenting, and domestic and family violence issues to name a few.

WHAT IS SEPARATION?

More often than not separation will mean a physical separation, but that is not always the case. At law, **separation** involves the irretrievable breakdown of the marital or de facto relationship. There must be an intention by one or both of the parties to end the relationship.

It is possible for parties to be separated and remain living under one roof. This is sometimes done out of convenience, or to maintain the living arrangements for the children with minimal disruption.

What is required is the communication of the intention to separate by one or both of the parties.

While considering what it means at law for you to be separated, it is also important to consider, in the context of a de facto relationship, whether you are in or have been in a de facto relationship and whether the principles in **Chapter 2** apply. Go back and have another look at **Chapter 2** for a rundown on when a de facto relationship exists.

IMPORTANT TIMEFRAMES

Before we dive into the different parts of the law, it is important to note the following very important timeframes. These timeframes relate to property settlement and the time limit within which you must bring your application (if you are unable to reach agreement).

If you are **married**, you must finalise your property settlement or bring a property application **within 12 months of your divorce becoming finalised**. In circumstances where you must wait 12 months and 1 day to file your divorce application (more about that in **Chapter 5**) it means that you have about 2 years and 3–4 months to sort out your property settlement, if you filed your divorce application immediately upon being able to.

If you are in a **de facto relationship,** you must finalise your property settlement or bring a property application within **2 years** of the end of your de facto relationship. Where there is a dispute about whether a relationship existed or when separation occurred, it is important to act quickly.

If you are contemplating separation or are separated, it is important to understand the family law process and some of the terminology used. In this chapter we dive into the detail of family law. We look at some general principles about what it means to separate, whether you are married or in a de facto relationship. There generally are four key things to consider:

- how your property will be divided;
- what income you might need to receive to meet your expenses;
- what the arrangements will be for your children, if you have children; and
- what support you might need for the children living with you.

There is information to consider when dividing property, or when seeking maintenance or spouse support. There are also factors to take into account when working through what arrangements are best for your children and whether you need support for any children living with you.

PROPERTY MATTERS

Putting to one side for the time being whether there is a dispute about the existence of a relationship, after a relationship has ended the property of the relationship needs to be divided. It is understandable that you may wish to divide the property between you and your ex-partner as soon as possible and simply move on with your life. The idea of dividing property may seem deceptively simple, but it is important to understand that there are likely hidden issues you could miss that will lead to complications or costs down the road.

There is no immediate rush to separate your property following separation, and you should be careful not to be pressured into making quick decisions, particularly if you haven't received any legal advice. The key timeframes to keep in mind are that property settlement proceedings have to be *started* or a formal agreement reached within 12 months of your divorce order becoming final; or, if you were de facto partners, within 2 years following your separation.

What is property?

Property includes a range of items, and it is important to determine exactly what property needs to be divided. Property is not just any money, houses and possessions you and your ex-partner own, but can also include investments, entitlements, superannuation, businesses and trusts.

Property will also include any liabilities – money you or your ex-partner owe, loans and tax obligations – and it will need to be decided how these will be repaid and/or who will be responsible for them.

How is property divided?

Property is either divided by agreement between you and your ex-partner, which can be done by negotiation with each other or through your lawyers. If you and your ex-partner cannot agree on the division of property after making a genuine attempt to do so, you may need to make an application for a court order on how the property is to be divided.

There is no stock-standard approach that the court takes when dividing property; rather, the process is guided by different factors that are taken into consideration. These include the contributions that each party makes to property and an assessment of the needs they will have in the future. Let's have a look at some of the main factors.

The legal framework

The legal framework to be applied when the court determines your property matter, whether a lawyer is assisting you to negotiate your matter or you are trying to work it out yourself, is set out in Part 8 (married couples) and Part 8AB (de facto couples) of the *Family Law Act*, along with the body of case law developed over the past almost 50 years. The law as it relates to married and de facto couples when working out their property settlement has essentially the same approach and process, just set out in different sections of the *Family Law Act*.

While there is an initial legal obligation to consider whether dividing the property of the relationship is just and equitable, in practical terms there is a longstanding four-step process to determine a property matter. This process is applied whether you are negotiating your outcome through lawyers, attending mediation or having the court decide your matter. Your family lawyer will also use these steps when providing you with advice about your matter.

The four-step exercise is as follows:

1. The court should determine what property there is and what value each property item has – this includes assets, liabilities, superannuation and financial resources (such as a company car);
2. The court should determine and assess the contributions that each party made to the property of the relationship and work out the entitlement of each party expressed as a percentage of the net value of the property of the parties;
3. The court should consider relevant matters including earning capacity, child support and any other orders made as well as those factors in section 75(2) (referred to below) so far as they are relevant;
4. Finally, the court should consider the overall effect of the

decision made, make orders and ensure that the distribution of property is just and equitable in all the circumstances of the case.

So what does this all mean?

To break down the law into plain English, first you need to work out what there is to divide between you. To do this, you think about what property you have with reference to the points above. The value of the property is assessed at the time of your negotiations, mediation or court hearing – it is not assessed at the date of separation.

The second step relates to:

- who brought what property (if any) into the relationship;
- how both parties contributed to the property of the relationship whether owned before, during or after the relationship;
- whether the contribution was financial, a gift or a windfall, money from a damages claim, lotto winnings or an inheritance, whether parents provided money to give the couple a hand during the relationship and the like;
- whether the contribution was non-financial and improved or maintained the property – perhaps one party was a builder by trade and both parties saved money by the time and effort put in by that party to build or improve property; perhaps one party was responsible for the upkeep of the garden and the other for the inside tasks like ironing, cooking, cleaning; perhaps all of these tasks were shared;
- any contributions made to the property of the parties by the parties after separation;
- the contributions made by a party or both of them to raising the children or caring for the home.

After working through this second step, an assessment in percentage terms is made of the parties' respective contributions to the relationship. Some important points to note are:

- there is no starting point of equality;
- a contribution as homemaker is not recognised in a token way but in a substantial way;
- there is no one-size-fits-all assessment.

The third step involves an assessment of the ongoing needs of the parties and the effect that any orders made or agreement reached might have on them. Here you need to consider:

- whether any order made is going to affect the earning capacity of either party to the relationship;
- the matters set out in section 75(2) of the *Family Law Act*;
- whether there is any other agreement or order in place that might impact this agreement or vice versa; and
- what the child support arrangements for the children are or should be.

Let's take a closer look at the abovementioned section 75(2). The *Family Law Act* establishes in this section a list of factors that should be considered to determine the ongoing needs of the parties. There are some factors that will apply to your matter and some that won't. The main ones that come up as they relate to property settlement are:

- the age of the parties and whether they have any health issues that affect their ability to earn income;

- the income, property and financial resources that the parties have or will receive;
- the capacity of each party to earn an income in appropriate gainful employment and whether the length of the relationship or circumstances of the relationship have affected a party's ability to earn income;
- whether one or both of the parties have the care of children of the relationship;
- the commitment of each party to support themselves, a child or another person including those in any new marriage or de facto relationship of either party;
- whether one or both of the parties receive a pension, allowance or benefit from Centrelink or a superannuation fund;
- whether there is a pre-existing financial agreement (such as a prenuptial agreement) that deals with how property will be divided on separation.

After assessing those factors, consideration is made as to whether there needs to be an adjustment to the percentage set after the second step: that is, should the percentage be adjusted in one person's favour to take into account that their capacity to earn an income is less than the other person's, or because they have greater care of the children?

The fourth and final step requires the court to stand back, have a look at the proposed orders and consider in all the circumstances whether the orders are just and equitable.

As you can see from the previous section, property matters upon separation are quite complicated. There are a number of factors that need to be considered and there is certainly no one answer that fits all cases.

SPOUSE MAINTENANCE

Following the end of your relationship you may find that with your household income no longer pooled, you are now unable to support yourself. In those circumstances it may be that you require some short-term financial support from your ex-spouse to top up any income that you may be receiving, or to be provided with income if you have no source of income. The purpose of maintenance in this form is to allow the party receiving the maintenance to re-establish themselves, usually over a period of two to three years.

The law that relates to maintenance is found in section 72 of the *Family Law Act* along with reference to section 75(2), which is also considered in determining property settlement.

Importantly, the requirements for spouse maintenance have two stages. First, the spouse requiring support needs to establish they have a need for maintenance in circumstances where they are unable to support themselves adequately because they have the care of a child from the relationship, they are unable to work or another adequate reason. In undertaking the assessment, reference is to be made to those factors listed in section 75(2). If, and only if, it can be established that a need exists, the second stage looks at whether the person who is to pay the maintenance has the capacity to do so.

In summary, the matters to be taken into consideration when assessing spouse maintenance are:

- the age and state of health of the parties;
- any income, property and financial resources available to the parties;
- the physical and mental capacity of the parties to work in appropriate gainful employment;
- whether a party is looking after a child from the relationship;

- whether completing a course or additional training would allow a party to get back into the workforce;
- the duration of the marriage and whether the duration has impacted the earning capacity of a party;
- whether either party is living with someone else; and
- any child support obligations.

Not all of the above matters will apply to every case. Which factors will apply will depend on the particular circumstances of your case. It is crucial to get legal advice before raising issues in court, as some factors will be more relevant than others and it may be wise to exercise discretion.

To work out if you are likely to need financial assistance from your spouse following separation, you should consider the following:

- Review what regular income you have available from various sources, e.g. work, Centrelink, other pensions;
- Go through your budget of things that you will now be paying for on your own – you might be paying rent, or the whole mortgage, electricity bills, phone bills, etc.;
- Note separately what expenses you have for the children, as these will always be considered separately to any expenses that you have for yourself;
- If your average weekly income is less than your expenses, you might be entitled to maintenance from your spouse and should seek some legal advice about your particular circumstances.

Unless there is a significant disparity between your income and that of your spouse – for example, one earns significantly more than the other, or one spouse has been out of the workforce looking after children or the home while the other has been working – maintenance arrangements are rare. You must have evidence that establishes your inability to support yourself adequately and you must consider making any request for maintenance, or application, soon after separation.

PARENTING MATTERS

There is a greater need for certainty in post-separation arrangements when there are children involved. There is a broad range of considerations, and it is wise to consult an experienced family lawyer as the legal process involved in determining a parenting agreement can be complex.

In addition to paternal and maternal instincts going into overdrive, matters involving children, as distinct from matters relating to property settlement, mean not only applying the established legal principles but also considering the dimension of social science and child development, which are overlaid with complicated emotional dynamics.

What the law says about parenting matters

At the outset, it is important to know there is a review underway with the intention of coming up with a simplified framework for parents and the courts when determining parenting arrangements. The information below is correct as at printing (in 2023). Information about the proposed amendments can be found towards the end of this section.

The law recognises the importance of providing stability and a positive environment for children, and the *Family Law Act 1975* sets out the way in which the law ensures the best interests of the child are protected.

Part 7 of the *Family Law Act 1975* contains the legal framework to be applied when dealing with your parenting matter. It is the framework and rules that the court applies. It is also the framework and rules that your lawyer must apply when giving you advice or managing your case with you.

The objects and principles of Part 7 of the *Family Law Act* are set out in section 60B.

The objects are to ensure that the best interests of children are met by:

- ensuring that children have the benefit of both of their parents having a meaningful involvement in their lives, to the maximum extent consistent with the best interests of the child; and
- protecting children from physical or psychological harm from being subjected to, or exposed to, abuse, neglect or family violence;
- ensuring that children receive adequate and proper parenting to help them achieve their full potential; and
- ensuring that parents fulfil their duties, and meet their responsibilities, concerning the care, welfare and development of their children.

The principles underlying these objects are:

- children have the right to know and be cared for by both their parents, regardless of whether their parents are married, separated, have never married or have never lived together;
- children have a right to spend time on a regular basis with, and communicate on a regular basis with, both their parents and other people significant to their care, welfare and development (such as grandparents and other relatives);
- parents jointly share duties and responsibilities concerning the care, welfare and development of their children;

- parents should agree about the future parenting of their children;
- children have a right to enjoy their culture, including the right to enjoy that culture with other people who share that culture.

The objects and principles are subject to the proviso that they should apply *except* if it would not be in a child's best interests to do so.

How are the children's best interests determined?

The factors that assist the court in determining what is in a child's best interests are set out in section 60CC. Those factors are broken up into primary considerations and additional considerations.

The primary considerations are:

- the benefit to the child of having a meaningful relationship with both of the child's parents; and
- the need to protect the child from physical or psychological harm from being subjected to, or exposed to, abuse, neglect or family violence.

These primary considerations were amended in 2012 following the introduction of significant reforms relating to family violence. It is for this reason that in applying the above two considerations, the court must give greater weight to the need to protect the child from harm.

There are a number of additional factors (also in section 60C) that must be considered, some of which include:

- any views expressed by the child balanced with the child's maturity and level of understanding;
- the child's relationship with each of their parents and significant others;

- the effect any changes to the child's circumstances might have on the child;
- any practical difficulties or expenses arising from the child spending time with either of the parents;
- the parent's capacity to provide for the needs of the child;
- the child's right to enjoy Aboriginal or Torres Strait Islander culture;
- family violence.

Which factors the court will consider in a matter will depend on the particular circumstances of each case. Again, it is crucial to get legal advice before raising issues in court, as some factors will be more relevant than others depending on the circumstances and it may be wise to exercise discretion.

How do you make decisions for your children?

The *Family Law Act* states that each parent has **parental responsibility** for a child under the age of 18 years (61C) and that parental responsibility means all the duties, powers, responsibilities and authority which, by law, parents have in relation to children (61B).

Importantly, there is a presumption that it is in the best interests of a child for the parents to have **equal shared parental responsibility** (61DA). This is not a reference to equal time. It is a reference to making big decisions about your child together. Big decisions include determining where your children will go to school, whether your children need significant medical intervention, the religion your children will practise and what name your children will be known by. Big decisions also include a decision to move further away from the other parent, thus making it more difficult for the children to spend time with that other parent. These issues are called **major long-term issues**. A parent's decision to enter into a new relationship is not by itself considered to be a major long-term issue.

This presumption for equal shared parental responsibility can be challenged in limited circumstances, depending on the circumstances of your matter. The presumption does not apply where there has been abuse of either the child in question or another child who was a member of the family, or family violence.

Less important decisions that are made on a daily basis will not require a joint decision or consultation. These include decisions about daily activities like when bedtime is or what the children should eat (unless there is an agreement based on an allergy or food intolerance) or whether they attend a friend's birthday party that falls on the same day as when the children are spending time with you.

What about the time your children spend with each parent?

The court sets out a reasonably straightforward but very wordy framework for determining the living arrangements for children. The framework is based on the presumption of equal shared parental responsibility being applied either by agreement or court order.

In summary, the *Family Law Act* in section 65DAA says the following:

- if the parents are to have equal shared parental responsibility for a child, the court must consider whether the child spending **equal time** with each of the parents is in the best interests of the child and reasonably practicable, and if so, make an order for equal time;
- if it is determined that it is not in the child's best interests, or reasonably practicable, the court must consider whether the child spending **substantial and significant time** is in the best

interests of the child and reasonably practicable, and if so, make an order for substantial and significant time;

- again, if that same determination is not made, the court must consider making **such other orders having regard to the best interests of the child**.

Substantial and significant time means time spent with the other parent on weekdays, weekends and holidays. The amount of time each parent spends with the child should allow them to be involved in both daily routines and significant events. In essence, most types of days for a child are covered including holidays, birthdays, Christmas and other special days. This reflects the law's attempt to make sure that both parents are able to be involved in their child's life in a variety of ways.

The court will consider whether the arrangements are **reasonably practical** by looking at factors such as:

- the distance between the parents' houses;
- each parent's capacity to implement the arrangements;
- each parent's current and future capacity to communicate with each other if difficulties arise;
- the likely impact of the arrangements on the child.

So what does this all mean?

Before you start to worry about whether your very young children will spend equal time with both parents or whether your teenager will cope better living in just one household through Years 11 or 12, there are some considerations you should keep in mind.

While it is not explicit in the sections set out above, the age of the children is important in several practical ways.

Firstly, **there is no magic age** at which your child can decide the living arrangements. By law, a child is a child until they turn 18, and you, as the child's parent, make decisions about them until they turn 18. That said, you might remember from earlier in the chapter that one of the factors the court considers when assessing the best interests of a child is any views expressed by the child balanced with the child's maturity and their level of understanding about their views. When assessing whether to take into account the views of a child, the age of the child is relevant. The child could be, for example, a mature and intelligent nine-year-old with a good understanding of what works in their life. Or they could be a thirteen-year-old who is childish or petulant in their dealings. It is for this reason that there is no one magic age where children take control.

Secondly, **the framework is subject to the best interests of the child**. Whether arrangements are reasonably practical requires an assessment of the impact on the child. This means that if it is not in the best interests of a newborn or very young child to be away from their primary carer, or the impact on the child will be to their detriment, it is unlikely that a court will make that order.

Ultimately, each parenting matter is different. There is no stock-standard answer to what your parenting arrangements should be. If, as parents, you cannot agree about what the arrangements for your children should be, it is really important that you get some legal advice about your particular circumstances.

Let's now turn to some other key points in parenting matters.

Family reports

If you are working towards resolving your matter or are in the middle of court proceedings, you may find yourself attending an interview for a **family report**. A family report interview is conducted by a family consultant who is usually either a social worker or a psychologist.

The family consultant will interview the parents and any extended family, and speak with the children if they are of an age where it is appropriate. The family consultant will then consider the evidence. This might be material provided by the parties, court documents or just the interviews themselves. They will consider, with regard to their own expertise and social science research, the competing proposals for each parent and make recommendations for parenting arrangements for the parents and court to consider.

Independent children's lawyers

In some matters, the court will appoint a lawyer to represent your children's best interests. This does not happen in all matters, but is more likely in the following instances:

- cases involving allegations of child abuse, whether physical, sexual or psychological;
- cases where there is an apparently intractable conflict between the parties;
- cases where the child is apparently alienated from one or both parents;
- cases where there are real issues of cultural or religious difference affecting the child;
- cases where the sexual preferences of either or both parents or some other person having significant contact with the child is likely to impinge on the child's welfare;
- where the conduct of either or both of the parents or some other person having significant contact with the child is alleged to be anti-social to the extent that it seriously impinges on the child's welfare;
- where there are issues of significant medical, psychiatric or

psychological illness or personality disorder affecting either party or a child or other person having significant contact with the child;

- any case in which, on the material filed by the parents, neither parent seems a suitable carer for the child;
- any case in which a child of mature years is expressing strong views that would involve changing a longstanding arrangement or a complete denial of contact to one parent;
- cases where one of the parties proposes that the child will either be permanently removed from the jurisdiction or permanently removed to such a place within the jurisdiction as to greatly restrict or exclude the other party from the possibility of contact with the child;
- cases where it is proposed to separate siblings;
- cases where neither party is legally represented;
- applications in the court's welfare jurisdiction relating in particular to the medical treatment of children where the child's interests are not adequately represented by one of the parties.

These factors come from a family law case called Re: K (1994) FLC 92-461.

Significantly, more than half of all applications filed will allege that risks exist for either parents or children. In the 2021–22 year, of all matters brought forward, 70% alleged that a child had been abused or was at risk of being abused, 80% alleged that a party had experienced family violence, 74% alleged that children had been exposed to family violence, 53% alleged that drug, alcohol or other substance misuse by a party had caused harm or posed a risk of harm to a child, and 58% alleged that the mental health issues of a party had caused harm or posed a risk of harm to a child. These are the types of matters in which an **independent children's lawyer** is ordinarily appointed.

If an independent children's lawyer is appointed in your matter, their role is to form a view as to what arrangements are best for your child or children, based on the evidence available. In their dealings the independent children's lawyer must act impartially, put any views of the children before the court, obtain and put before the court any reports that will assist the court in determining the arrangements, minimise trauma to the child and facilitate, where possible, an agreed resolution if doing so is in the best interests of the child. The role of the independent children's lawyer is set out in the *Family Law Act* at section 68LA(5).

What are the proposed amendments to the *Family Law Act*?

The Australian Government is currently consulting on proposed changes to the *Family Law Act* that will simplify the assessment of what arrangements are in a child's best interests. As you have read earlier in this section, the current system requires that a presumption of equal shared parental responsibility (decision making) be applied, which then requires the court to first consider equal time, then substantial and significant time, followed by other time, all with reference to the 2 primary and 13 additional best-interest factors.

One of the most commonly misunderstood parts of the law relating to parenting matters lies in the presumption of equal shared parental responsibility. It is often thought that the presumption relates to equal time, and that it is the right or entitlement of parents to have an equal time arrangement.

The consultation papers issued by the Australian Government propose that the legislation be amended by:

- removing the presumption of equal shared parental responsibility and the framework regarding equal time and substantial and significant time;
- simplifying the current best-interest factors to 6 factors (instead of the 2 primary and 13 additional);
- including a standalone factor to emphasise the importance of keeping a connection to culture for Aboriginal and Torres Strait Islander children;
- including the factors to consider when a parenting arrangement can be changed. These factors are currently provided for within case law rather than within the *Family Law Act*. The intention is to provide a clear list of the factors that a court should look at when deciding whether final parenting orders should be reconsidered;
- adding a requirement, in the majority of cases, for an Independent Children's Lawyer to meet with children to make sure their views are considered when the court makes parenting arrangements, and removing the requirement that ICLs are only appointed in exceptional circumstances in matters relating to the Hague Convention on the Civil Aspects of International Child Abduction;
- simplifying the section relating to the contravention and enforcement of parenting orders;
- making it clearer when information about proceedings can be shared – section 121 of the Act prohibits the sharing of information to protect the privacy of families and children; however, there is often confusion about how far this protection extends;
- adding protections from the misuse of the family law system by perpetrators of family violence through excessive applications and issue of subpoenas for personal medical information; and

- establishing standards and requirements for report writers who undertake family assessments.

Links to these consultation papers can be found in the **Bibliography** at the end of the book.

There are some welcome changes in the simplification of the framework for parenting arrangements, particularly if it helps to remove the common misconception about an automatic 'right' to equal time. Added protections in the sharing of information and the safeguarding of family violence victims will build on the 2012 and 2019 reforms in this area, which brought to the forefront of participants in the family law system the need to protect children from psychological and physical harm caused by neglect, abuse or family violence. It is still early days and the final draft may look very different to the changes proposed.

CHILD SUPPORT

If you have separated from your partner and have care of the child/children from that relationship, you will likely be able to apply for financial assistance from the other parent in the form of **child support**.

Child support is an ongoing payment from one parent to the other, for the financial benefit of a child from that relationship. The payment of child support represents the recognition that both parents have a responsibility to provide for their children, and makes sure that a child is supported financially by both their parents.

Why do we have child support?

The child support scheme applies to all parents, in that both parents of a child have the primary duty to maintain the child. The child support legislation states that the duty of a parent to maintain a child has priority over all commitments of the parent other than those commitments that enable the parent to support themselves or any other children the parent has a duty to maintain.

The principal object of the child support legislation is to ensure that children receive a proper level of financial support from their parents.

Who can apply for child support?

The parent with whom the child is living after separation is the one who lodges the application for child support. This is done through the Child Support Agency, not the family court system.

Parents of children from same-sex relationships are able to apply for child support provided they are able to reach the legal requirements relating to parentage. Generally, these requirements will be reached if the child:

- was adopted by the couple;
- was conceived by an artificial conception procedure, and the parents were in a de facto relationship at time of conception; or
- was born through a surrogacy arrangement and there is a court order declaring the couple to be the child's parents.

Non-parent carers may also be able to apply for child support from both of the child's parents. A non-parent can be someone other than the parent who cares for the child, such as a grandparent or other family member, or a legal guardian. You are able to apply for child support if you care for the child 128 nights or more in the year, and are not in a domestic relationship with either of the parents. This is done by submitting a Non-Parent Carer application with the Child Support Agency.

After lodging your application, you will receive an assessment notice that states how much is to be received/paid each month, and your rights relating to these payments. You can then choose the most appropriate method for collecting this child support.

If a parent is receiving a pension or benefit from Centrelink, that parent will be required to apply for a child support assessment through the Child Support Agency, otherwise, the pension or benefit may be reduced.

How long does the obligation last?

The obligation to pay child support continues until a child turns 18 years of age, or to the conclusion of Year 12 if the child turns 18 in that year of schooling (noting that a specific application must be made to continue the child support through to the conclusion of Year 12).

How is child support calculated?

The procedure for paying and receiving child support is governed by the *Child Support (Assessment) Act 1989* and the *Child Support (Registration and Collection) Act 1988*.

The Acts provide a mathematical formula for determining how much child support or maintenance you will have to pay, or will receive. Child support is regulated by the Child Support Agency, not by the family court.

The actual process of assessing the amount of child support can be quite complex, but in general terms it involves calculating the percentage of care each parent provides, determining if a parent is not meeting their entire share of the costs of the child through such care, then calculating the amount of child support they should be paying, based on the combined incomes of both parents.

Factors that are relevant to determining child support rates include:

- the income of the parents;
- how many children are involved;
- the amount of time the child spends with each parent;
- the level of care each parent provides for the child;
- the amount of money each parent needs to support themselves;
- other dependent children either parent has responsibility for.

In practical terms, the simplest way to work out your child support liability or the payment you are to receive is through the Department of Human Services Child Support Estimator. The estimator takes you through the above points and prepares a calculation based on your circumstances. You can find it by typing 'child support estimator' into your web search engine and it should direct you to the Child Support Agency website.

How do you pay or receive child support?

There are different methods of organising and managing your child support payments. How you choose to arrange this will largely depend on your personal circumstances, particularly how well you are able to communicate with your ex-partner.

You are not bound by your choice and are able to change to another arrangement later on if you wish. Importantly, the parent who is receiving the child support needs to agree to the collection method.

Child support collection involves the Child Support Agency assessing the amount to be paid, and then collecting and transferring that amount between the parents. There is no need for direct contact between the parents, which may be necessary for a variety of reasons. The agency has enforcement options if the payments are not being made; it will also maintain records on the payments and you will be required to inform it about changes in your circumstances.

Private collection allows you to make/collect your child support payments privately. You and the other parent come to an agreement about the most convenient or appropriate payment method for both of you. You still pay or receive the amount the Child Support Agency assessed, but you have the flexibility to arrange the payments whenever and however you wish. You will need to keep your own records of the payment; if payments are not being made, you may need to seek assistance from the Child Support Agency to enforce them.

The **self-managed** option means you and the other parent decide on the amount to be paid, as well as when and how it should be paid. You manage the payments yourself and do not need to register with the Child Support Agency. While this method allows you to have full control over the arrangements, it also means that any unpaid money cannot be collected by the Agency and you are responsible for your own records of payment.

If you and the other parent are not able to communicate effectively, it is probably best for you to organise your child support through the Child Support Agency and to opt for the Child Support Collect method. This may also be a preferable option if either of you needs a structure to ensure the payments are made on time.

Documenting your child support agreement

If you have reached an agreement about child support collection privately or are managing the collection of child support yourself, you should still document the agreement so that it is clear what each parent's obligations are. In legal terms, a child support agreement can be either a limited one or a binding one. You can download a limited child support agreement from the Department of Human Services Child Support Agency. You'll find the website details in the **Resources** section at the back of this book.

Otherwise, you can visit a family lawyer who can assist you with a limited child support agreement. Alternatively, you can talk to your family lawyer about a binding child support agreement. We'll discuss both the limited and binding child support agreements in the following section.

What sort of formal agreements regulate the payment of child support?

Aside from a formal assessment by the Child Support Agency, there are two types of formal agreements which set out the terms of any child support agreement:

A **limited child support agreement** is an agreement in writing setting out the child support arrangements. The child support payable must not be less than the child support that would be paid under an assessment. The agreement must be accepted by the Registrar of Child Support to be valid. There is no requirement for legal advice when entering into this type of agreement. The agreement is valid for a maximum of 3 years.

To prepare a limited child support agreement, you can either download the child support agreement form from the Department of Human Services (referred to above) or you can talk to your family lawyer. While there is no formal requirement to seek independent legal advice, the Child Support Agency recommends that you seek advice because the agreement may impact your rights and entail obligations, a subject we'll look at further below.

A **binding child support agreement** again is an agreement in writing that sets out the child support arrangements. A binding agreement differs from a limited agreement in that:

- before signing the binding child support agreement, you must receive independent legal advice about the effect the agreement has on your rights, and the advantages and disadvantages of entering into the agreement;

- your lawyer will sign a certificate confirming that you received this advice; the certificate is attached to the agreement;
- the agreement can be more or less than the amount of child support that would be paid under an assessment;
- the agreement must contain the formal requirements set out in the *Child Support (Assessment) Act*.

Advantages and disadvantages of child support agreements

While the advantages and disadvantages of entering into a child support agreement will always depend on the individual circumstances of the person, two key points are:

- One great advantage is that there is certainty in the amount of child support being paid or received. You have clarity about how much, when and the type of child support. It might be a cash sum, or there might be an agreement to pay the school fees. Either way, both parents have certainty about the arrangements.
- A common disadvantage is the binding nature of a binding child support agreement. It is generally drafted in a manner that makes it difficult to change if there is a significant change in circumstances. If, for example, one party is made redundant and has difficulty finding new work, if the other party does not agree to change the agreement, a court application is required.

Do child support matters ever go to court?

There are limited circumstances where child support arrangements go to court. Some examples include:

- cases where the paternity of the child is in dispute;
- if you are in proceedings for property or parenting matters and you want to suspend any assessment process pending the outcome of those proceedings;
- if you have property or parenting proceedings underway and you need to depart from an assessment that doesn't take into account your proper circumstances;
- if you want to set aside or vary a child support agreement but the other parent won't agree to stop or change the arrangements set out in the agreement.

Child support, Centrelink and family violence

Ordinarily, if you are separated and receiving a Family Tax Benefit you are obliged to take reasonable action to seek maintenance from the other parent. It is for this reason that when parents separate and one parent applies for a parenting payment from Centrelink, a child support assessment quickly follows. Parents who rely on Centrelink must take reasonable steps to seek maintenance from the other parent, rather than relying only on government payments.

Where family and domestic violence is a factor, the Child Support Agency recognises the risks to the receiving parent of further aggravating a serious situation. For that reason, a parent can apply for a full or partial exemption from the collection of child support without impacting the Family Tax Benefit received. If you find yourself in this situation, you should speak with the Department of Human Services, which provides social work services along with referrals to other services in the domestic and family violence network to support you and your family.

Chapter 4:

Domestic and family violence

If you need urgent assistance when you are experiencing domestic and family violence, you should contact 000 or 1800 RESPECT (737 732). Further local domestic and family violence services can be found in the Resources section of this book.

The law relating to domestic and family violence differs in each state. There are some key principles that are the same, but the governing law is different. It is not possible within the scope of this book to go through the law in each state, so it is important that you see a solicitor in your state if you need assistance with domestic and family violence.

The key definitions, however, are similar across the states. The accepted understanding of what is and isn't appropriate behaviour is, in my view, consistent across Australia.

In this section, I generally refer to the Queensland *Domestic and Family Violence Protection Act 2012*. The sections referred to in this chapter are found in this Act. Where comparison to other states can be made, I have included those. You should note the orders, each having the same purpose, in each state are:

- Protection Order (Queensland)
- Apprehended Violence Order (New South Wales)
- Family Violence Intervention Order (Victoria)
- Family Violence Order (Tasmania)
- Intervention Order (South Australia)
- Family Violence Restraining Order (Western Australia)
- Domestic Violence Order (Australian Capital Territory & Northern Territory)

It is important to note that you do not need a new application if you move to another state or territory. On 25 November 2017, laws came into force that automatically recognise protection orders from all states and territories. If your order was made before 25 November 2017, you can apply to have it registered in other states that you travel to frequently if you are concerned about your safety there.

WHAT IS DOMESTIC VIOLENCE?

Domestic violence has a broad definition and can range from physical or sexual assault to verbal, emotional and psychological abuse. Domestic violence can also take on other forms such as financial abuse, where one person limits the other's access to assets or money, usually as a way of controlling that person. Threats, coercion and other methods of control are also recognised forms of domestic violence.

If you are experiencing domestic violence, you can apply to your local magistrates court for a protection order. This is a different court from the Federal Circuit and Family Court of Australia.

PROTECTION ORDERS

A **protection order** sets out orders that restrain the respondent (the other party) from committing acts of domestic and family violence against the aggrieved (the person applying for protection). For example, this can include:

- orders not to commit domestic and family violence against the aggrieved or any other person named on the order, such as family or children;
- orders not to come into contact with the aggrieved, or within a certain distance of their home, work or other locations;
- orders not to communicate with the aggrieved, unless they are

going through family law separation and there is an agreement in writing for them to communicate about the children;

- other orders for the personal protection of the aggrieved.

What types of relationships are covered?

Section 13 of the Act states that a protection order can only be made where there is a domestic or family relationship between the parties. Examples include:

- **intimate personal relationship**, which includes current or former spouses or de facto partners, fiancé/fiancée, a 'couple relationship' such as girlfriend and boyfriend, and same-sex couples (section 14);
- **family relationship**, such as parent and child, siblings and other relatives who are connected by blood or marriage (section 19);
- **informal care relationship**, where a person is dependent on another person to help them in an activity of daily living; for example, dressing and grooming, meals and shopping and other functions of daily living (section 20).

Who can apply for a protection order?

If you have experienced domestic violence, you can report this to police and they may make the application for an order on your behalf. Alternatively, you can make an application yourself, without the assistance of police. You can also authorise someone to make an application on your behalf, such as a family member or friend; however, this person must be over 18 years of age.

How do I make an application for a protection order?

There is a specific **application form** to fill out. You can obtain this form from the police (if they are making the application on your behalf), your lawyer, the local magistrates court where you will lodge your application, or in some cases on the internet.

In Queensland, South Australia, Tasmania and Western Australia you can download the application form from that state's court website, and from the government website in the case of the Northern Territory.

Links to these forms can be found in the Resources section of this book.

In the following states/territories you need to go either to the police for assistance or to the local court or magistrates court:

- New South Wales;
- Victoria;
- Australian Capital Territory.

You will be referred to as the **aggrieved** or **applicant** or **protected person**. The other party will be referred to as the **respondent** or **defendant**. If you are making the application yourself, you or your lawyer should complete the form and file it at your nearest magistrates court. You can ask the court to put certain 'conditions' on the order, if one is made, such as that the respondent cannot come to your house or place of work, or cannot contact you. When your application is filed, the court will give you a date that you (and your lawyer, if you have one) will have to appear to have the application considered in the first instance. This will usually take place that day or within the next couple of days, and is usually heard **ex parte**, which is a legal term meaning 'without the other party there'.

Police Protection Notice

The Queensland Police have the power to issue a Police Protection Notice (PPN). The PPN is an immediate protection order in place to protect a named aggrieved from a named respondent, pending a formal court application. The PPN can be issued if the police reasonably believe the respondent has committed domestic violence, an attempt to speak to the respondent has been made, no protection order exists, it is necessary and desirable to protect the aggrieved and there is no intention to take the respondent into custody (section 101).

The PPN is often handwritten by a police officer called to a domestic violence incident where the circumstances require the notice to be issued and subsequently followed by a formal application by the police in the coming days.

What happens at the first court date?

The court hearing is always **closed** when matters concerning protection orders are heard. This means that only the police, the parties and their legal representatives are allowed inside the courtroom. If you do not have a lawyer, the court may allow you to have a support person. The magistrate will consider your application. If the magistrate considers it necessary, they will make a **Temporary Protection Order** (TPO) that will state certain conditions depending on the circumstances. For example, the TPO may require that the respondent be of good behaviour towards the aggrieved and not commit acts of domestic violence, or that they remain a certain distance from the aggrieved and the place where the aggrieved lives, works or frequents. It is then the job of the police to serve your application and the TPO (if one is made) on the respondent. The TPO is not in effect until it is served on the respondent. A second court date will be set.

What happens after the respondent is served with my application?

The respondent may be at the next court event, and will be asked if they consent to the protection order being made. Sometimes the respondent will agree to the order being made **without admissions**, on certain conditions, which means that they do not admit that there have been any acts of domestic violence, but they consent to all or part of the order in any event. If the respondent does not attend, the court will consider making the order final provided the respondent has been served.

If the order is consented to

If the respondent consents to the order being made, the magistrate will make that order, usually to remain in place for 5 years, unless otherwise agreed by the parties or unless the magistrate can be convinced that a shorter time period should apply (such as 2 years).

If the order is not consented to

If the respondent does not consent to the order being made, or does not agree to the conditions of the order, the matter is set down for a hearing. If there is a TPO in place, the magistrate will usually extend that order until the matter goes to that hearing. If there is no TPO, the magistrate can make one, or decide not to make one and wait until the matter is decided on a final basis at the hearing. The magistrate will make a **directions order** that sets out certain dates. The first date will be a date by which the applicant must file their own **affidavit**, along with any affidavits from witnesses that will support their case and give evidence at the hearing. An **affidavit** is a sworn written statement that is filed in court and used in court proceedings, such as hearings. The respondent will then have to file their affidavit. There may also be a **compliance hearing** to make sure the matter is ready to proceed.

What happens at the hearing?

At the protection order hearing, the parties bring the matter before the magistrate and present their application and defence, and support their positions with evidence such as affidavit material and witnesses. The magistrate will consider all the relevant evidence and make a decision in accordance with the *Domestic and Family Violence Protection Act 2012* (Qld). The magistrate will then decide whether or not to make an order and what conditions are to be imposed by any order made.

The applicant will present their evidence and witnesses first. The applicant and their witnesses will then be cross-examined by the respondent's lawyer or barrister. If the respondent does not have legal representation, they may undertake this cross-examination themselves. The applicant may understandably be upset by this, especially where they have been the victim of severe abuse. Unlike at the Federal Circuit and Family Court of Australia, where cross-examination banning orders can be made stopping a respondent from cross-examining a victim in person, those arrangements do not apply in Queensland protection order matters.

In those circumstances, the applicant may ask the court to make different arrangements for giving evidence under cross-examination. This can include giving evidence from a different courtroom by video link, the use of a screen so that the victim is unable to see the respondent, having the respondent appear via a separate courtroom or having a support person (section 150). You may want to ask your lawyer about this.

In Victoria, laws exist to prevent the respondent from directly questioning the aggrieved.

The respondent will then present their defence and put forward a case that either there have not been acts of domestic violence, or that the order is not necessary or desirable. The applicant will be entitled to cross-examine the respondent to test their case.

Who can be a witness?

You can ask other people to provide evidence for you to help you at the hearing. If someone agrees to provide evidence, that witness must make themselves available on the day of the hearing. If the witness provides an affidavit but does not make themselves available for cross-examination on the day of the hearing, the court can decide how much weight, if any, it will give to the affidavit material.

What if the respondent breaches the protection order?

Breaching the order means that the respondent has done something that is against the terms of the order. For example, if the order states that the respondent cannot approach the aggrieved within 100 metres but then does so, this may be a breach of the order. The aggrieved should report this to the police and the police will investigate the incident.

If the respondent commits an act of domestic violence that is in and of itself a criminal act – a physical assault, for example – they will be charged both for the assault and for breaching the order.

If the police are satisfied that an offence and/or a breach of the order has occurred, they will either arrest and charge the respondent, or serve the respondent with a **Notice to Appear** in court to answer the charge or charges. These breach proceedings are criminal in nature and therefore heard in an open court, except in limited circumstances.

If the respondent pleads guilty to the offence and/or the breach of the order, they will then be sentenced. The punishment will depend on many factors, including the seriousness of the offence and the respondent's criminal record. If the respondent pleads not guilty to the charge or charges, the matter will go to a hearing.

What if the respondent breaches a temporary protection order (TPO)?

If there is a TPO in place, and the respondent has been served with that TPO by police, the respondent can still be found to have breached the order (even though it is a temporary order).

What do I do if the order is going to expire and I still want it in place?

You can apply to the court to have the order extended. The court will extend an order if you can show that it is necessary and desirable to do so.

Our circumstances have changed and I want to vary the order

Sometimes parties can work things out and in those circumstances you might like to apply to the court to have the conditions of an order varied or withdrawn. This may be more difficult if the order was made on a police application.

I am a respondent to an application – what should I do?

It is likely that the first you will know about an application is when either the applicant tells you, or when you are served with the application by the police. The application and any temporary order will be explained to you. You will be advised of the next court date.

At the next court date you will have three options:

- You can seek an adjournment for the purposes of seeking legal advice, if you have not already had the opportunity to do so.
- You can consent to the order. You can do this **without admissions**, which means that you do not admit that there have been any acts of domestic violence, but you consent to the order in any event. This will end the matter before the court.

- You can choose not to consent to the order. The matter will be set down for a hearing.

If you do not attend court, the court will consider making the order final provided you have been served.

You should seek legal advice about the effect that a protection order has on you before you consent to an order.

Chapter 5:

Divorce and ending your de facto relationship

In this chapter, you will find information about formally ending your relationship, whether it be a marriage or a de facto situation. It is a difficult and challenging time for most people, so I have set out below some basic practical matters to keep in mind when you are going through this process.

The process for formally ending your marriage is done through an application for a **divorce order**. The divorce order is the formal record that your marriage has ended. The ending of your de facto relationship does not require a court application. If you have not registered your relationship you don't need to take any formal steps. If you have formally registered your de facto relationship, you can lodge a form at the Births, Deaths and Marriages registry in your state, which formally ends the registration of your relationship.

DIVORCE (FORMALLY ENDING YOUR MARRIAGE)

The word **divorce** can be seen as an all-encompassing term to describe the separation process – 'I'm getting a divorce', 'my cousin Max is getting divorced'. A lot of lawyers also describe themselves as a 'divorce lawyer'.

Technically, however, an **application for divorce** is an administrative application to the court to formally end your marriage on the record; the application results in a divorce order. In the same way that you receive a marriage certificate when you marry, you receive a **divorce certificate** once your divorce order has become final. In this section a divorce order is referred to as a divorce.

Applying for a divorce is totally separate from a parenting or property matter. It does not impact in any way your parenting arrangements for your children. It may impact your property settlement in certain circumstances.

You can apply for a divorce one year and one day after you formally separate from your husband or wife. You must have lived separately and apart for a period of at least 12 months, with no reasonable likelihood of a reconciliation. You must have either agreed on a separation date or clearly communicated to your spouse that you consider the marriage to be over.

You must be an Australian citizen, domiciled in Australia (that is, you treat Australia as your home) and ordinarily resident in Australia for at least 12 months prior to filing the application.

If you have lived separately for at least 12 months, the process is relatively easy. Where you have lived under one roof but separately, or where you have got back together and separated again, there will be some extra documents you need to prepare. You might also need to get some advice from a lawyer about this. The easiest thing to do, of course, is to just wait until you have been living apart for 12 months. Obviously there might be some circumstances where that isn't possible, so seeking advice on this point from a lawyer is crucial.

Over time the process for applying for a divorce has become more refined and streamlined. The Federal Circuit and Family Court of Australia (the court responsible for divorce applications) now runs entirely electronic court files for divorce applications. You cannot go to the court registry to file an application for divorce in person. Applications are lodged online through the Commonwealth Courts Portal. Any supporting documents are uploaded through the Portal. All court events are conducted by telephone.

The divorce process

Separation.

Lodge application.

Serve application.

Divorce hearing.

Divorce final.

Before you file your divorce application you need to consider whether you are making the application on your own, or whether you and your spouse agree to make a joint application. There are some benefits to a joint application that you need to consider:

- If you make a joint application, you do not need to appear before the court on the hearing date. On the hearing date, the court will check the application and, provided you have complied with the administrative requirements, grant your divorce order.
- You may be able to share the fees associated with filing the application with your former partner.
- You don't have to arrange to **serve** (provide a copy of) the divorce application on your spouse. (We'll discuss further what is meant by service below.)

At the time of printing of this book, the filing fee to apply for a divorce is $1,060. If you have a Centrelink concession card such as a pensioner concession card or health care card, you can seek a reduction of the fee to $350. If you are making a joint application, both parties must have a concession card to take advantage of the reduced filing fee.

In comparison, if you are making a sole divorce application:

- At the time of lodging your application you will be allocated a hearing date. This is typically 8–12 weeks from the time you lodge the application.
- Once you have lodged the application, you will need to arrange to serve (provide a copy to) your spouse.
- Service must occur 28 days prior to your hearing date.
- If you have children, you must appear before the court on the hearing date.

- If you don't have children, and you have lodged your affidavit proving service, you don't have to appear before the court on the hearing date.

What is 'service'?

Service is one of those legal terms which can be quite confusing. It is very different, for example, from the service you might receive at a store or a nice restaurant. For applications to proceed before the court, they usually must be personally served on the other party. So what is **personal service**?

Service involves your court application being given to the other party. This is usually undertaken by a third party, either someone you know or someone whose job it is to serve documents such as a service agent. The documents are personally handed to the other person by that third party – not by you.

Alternatively, the court allows you to post a copy of the divorce application to the other party, but they must sign a form that confirms they received the application.

For an application to proceed, you must prove to the court that the court documents have been personally given to the other party. The court will not make an order about another party if that party isn't aware of the application (there are some rare exceptions that aren't relevant to a divorce).

Once the application has been given to the other party, the person who served the documents for you must prepare an affidavit setting out the documents that were provided, confirm that they either knew or identified the person, and have them sign an acknowledgement confirming they received the documents.

In some circumstances, the party receiving the documents does not want to receive them or is being deliberately difficult. The person physically serving the application can still carry out their task by placing a copy at the foot of the other party and explaining the documents that are being presented to them. In this situation, though, it is best to consult with a family lawyer to make sure that you have complied with any service requirements.

The court hearing

It is not an automatic requirement that you go to court for the hearing of your application for divorce. If you have made a joint application, you do not need to attend court.

If you have made a sole application and you do not have children under 18 years of age and have completed documents confirming service of your application, you don't need to go to court. If you have made a sole application and have children, you will need to appear before the court for the hearing of the application.

If you have to appear before the court, your application will be heard by a registrar of the court. All divorce applications are heard by telephone. The registrar will go through all your documents and, if satisfied that everything is correct and in order, they will grant the divorce order. If you don't have to go to court, this process will occur administratively and, provided all the documents are completed properly, the registrar will grant the divorce order.

One month and one day after your divorce hearing, your divorce order will become final.

There is one key date flowing from the granting of your divorce order that you must keep in mind. Once your divorce order becomes final, you have 12 months within which to either:

- finalise your property settlement by financial agreement or consent order; or

- commence proceedings for property settlement or spouse maintenance orders.

This is very important to remember. If your property matter has not been finalised and is not before the court when your divorce order becomes final, you need to make a note of the date – you have 12 months to act before you will be prevented from commencing proceedings without first obtaining permission from the court.

As mentioned in **Chapter 2**, these are important timeframes that apply when your relationship ends. When you have your divorce order, the *Family Law Act* puts what can be seen as an 'end date' by when you must sort out your property settlement. This is so that matters do not go on and on for years after a marriage has formally ended, and so people can move on with their lives with certainty that another claim for property settlement will not be made.

Where your divorce is entirely an administrative process of formally ending your marriage, it is not necessary to wait for that application to be made to finalise your parenting and/or property matter. They are entirely separate processes.

ENDING YOUR DE FACTO RELATIONSHIP

Ending your de facto relationship does not have the same level of formality as ending a marriage. There is no court application to go through, and if you haven't registered your relationship, there are no formal steps that you need to take.

If you have registered your relationship, you need to apply to end or revoke that registration. This process is done through the Registry of Births, Deaths and Marriages in each state. Each state has an application form to complete.

You can lodge a joint application where both parties to the relationship complete the required form and register the form. Alternatively, you can lodge a sole application. You must complete a declaration that you have provided a copy of the application form to the other party. The registry office will not process the application if the other party does not know about the application.

You must arrange for personal delivery of the application to the other party. Unlike with an application for divorce, you can do this yourself. Alternatively, you can arrange for a third party to deliver the documents. You can also send the application form by registered post to their last known residential address.

Once the application has been given to the other party, the person who served the documents for you must prepare a declaration setting out the documents that were provided, and confirming that they either knew or identified the person and had them sign an acknowledgement confirming they received the documents. If the application was sent by post, the person who sent the post must prepare the declaration.

In some circumstances, the party receiving the documents may be resistant to receiving them. They can still be served by the person delivering the documents, who would place them at the foot of the party and explain what they are. If you are having difficulty in having the other party receive your documents, it is best to consult with a family lawyer to make sure that you have complied with any service requirements.

Each state in Australia has a different form to end the registration of a de facto relationship. The relevant link for each state can be found in the **Resources** section at the end of this book.

Chapter 6:

Going to court

Unless your matter involves complex abuse allegations, a desire by one party to relocate a significant distance away from the other with children or complicating factors requiring a specific determination by a judge, it is likely that your matter won't need to be determined by a judge. Only about 5–10% of all matters go before a judge for a final hearing. Most matters will resolve before getting to court or during the court process, usually through one of the alternative dispute resolution options such as mediation, set out in **Chapter 7**. For example, about 95% of matters going to mediation will resolve. Why wouldn't you take those odds? Armed with the knowledge you need to resolve your matter, surely it's best to grab that opportunity with both hands.

One of the greatest frustrations of our family law system has been the **delay** involved in waiting for matters to go to trial. The family law system is funded by the Commonwealth Government. Unfortunately, there is limited federal funding available to fund the court system, which means in turn that we have a shortage of judges available to hear and determine matters. A matter filed in the family court in 2017 that required determination by a judge was unlikely to be finally heard and determined until 2019 or even later.

It's all too evident that we have had a backlog in the system. Parties with matters that are awaiting a trial are being advised that there will be an 18-month to 2-year delay before their matter can be heard by a judge. That timeframe runs *after* you have been through all preliminary steps including any attempt to resolve the matter. Your life is in a holding pattern while you wait.

These delays, together with a duplicated court system, were significant factors behind the merging of our two family Courts in September 2021. The Family Court of Australia and the Federal Circuit Court of Australia merged to become the Federal Circuit and Family Court of Australia. Along with one set of court forms came a Central Practice Direction for the management of all family law matters before the Court. (Note that the Family Court of Western Australia remains a separate Court.)

The cases awaiting trial are not all about abuse and relocation. The other complicating factor is quite often **the personalities at play** – those who are stubborn in nature or just want their 'day in court'. There will always be competing personalities that won't be able to resolve their matter in a sensible way. It may be that this personality type is on the other side of your matter. Knowledge about this is a benefit, in a sense. Understanding the family law system and using it to your advantage with guidance from your family lawyer might make this process more bearable for you.

A third and important factor to consider is the **costs involved**. Aside from the time it takes to get through the court system, the costs involved in taking your matter all the way through to a final hearing can be high. While each matter is different and it's not possible to give an estimate of fees without understanding your particular matter, you can add up the following:

- Preparing your court material takes time. It will take several hours to pull together all the evidence relevant for your final hearing.
- Attending at the final hearing takes time; you also need to account for your barrister to prepare for and then attend on each day of the court hearing.
- If your matter runs for more than one day the costs are significant.

This should be compared to the costs you might pay to attend a private mediation (see **Chapter 7**) where the success rate is as high as 95%. Your family law solicitor will be able to give you a better indication of what these fees will be once they understand your matter.

Legal costs are a significant focus of the merged Court with parties required to disclose to the Court and the other party, by filing a costs notice, the amount of costs incurred so far, the costs to be incurred for the upcoming event and future costs if the matter does not resolve. These costs notices must be filed on each occasion the matter is before the Court. Judicial officers are very aware of what parties are spending. The Central Practice Direction notes that the Court expects parties and their lawyers to have in mind, at all times, the cost of each step in the proceedings and whether it is necessary, and to avoid unnecessary process-driven costs and unjustified use of court resources.

To appreciate the benefits of avoiding going to court, it is important to understand just what *is* involved in going to court. In this chapter, we'll look at the various steps involved in court proceedings.

BEFORE YOU FILE

Before you lodge your application with the court, there are procedures that you need to follow. Whether your matter relates to parenting or property or both, the rules that govern the family law courts require that you first make a genuine attempt to resolve your matter.

This step is compulsory for a parenting application. You must first attend a family dispute resolution or mediation session and attempt to resolve your matter. You can read more about those processes in **Chapter 7**. A family dispute resolution practitioner will work with both parties to assist them in reaching an agreement. If they are unable to reach an agreement, yet have made a genuine attempt to do so, a certificate is issued by the family dispute resolution practitioner. The family dispute resolution practitioner can also assess whether the matter is inappropriate for mediation, such as in the case of allegations of child abuse or domestic and family violence.

Before you lodge.

Make a genuine attempt to resolve the matter

Parenting Compulsory Family Dispute Resolution

Property Disclosure Exchange Offers Attend Mediation

Prepare court documents

Lodge court documents

6-8 weeks

Serve court documents on another party

Other party responds within 28 days of service

First court date

Information gathering and dispute resolution process

Interim hearing

Family report

Private Mediation

Court dispute resolution process - parenting or property

Second court date

The Court Process

When all interim
matters dealt with

Compliance and
Readiness Hearing

The trial

Decision 3-12 months

Appeal - lodged
within 28 days

Possible referral back for rehearing

Appeal hearing

Appeal decision

Once you have your certificate from the family dispute resolution practitioner, you can file your application. There are some circumstances where you can apply for an exemption from the family dispute resolution process. When you are lodging a new application, section 60I(9) provides for the following exemptions:

- where the matter is urgent;
- where there are allegations of child abuse or family violence;
- where one party is unable to participate in mediation due to incapacity of some kind, physical remoteness or some other reason.

There is no formal requirement for mediation in property matters before commencing proceedings, though in practice most good family lawyers will recommend that you go to mediation before lodging your application.

There is a requirement that, where it is possible, you let the other party know that you are going to commence proceedings. In property matters you should also make sure that you have **disclosed** (shared with the other party) all relevant documents to the other party. These documents generally are:

- bank statements for any individual or shared accounts for the past 12 months;
- your three most recently lodged tax returns and notices of assessment;
- your most recent group certificate if you did not lodge a tax return;
- three recent pay slips for your current job;
- a Centrelink payment or pension statement (if applicable);
- your most recent superannuation statement;

- valuations for any vehicles that you own including cars, motorbikes or any other form of transport;
- valuations of any property individually owned by you or jointly owned with someone else;
- documents relating to any companies or trust structures including financial statements for those companies and trusts where you are a director, shareholder, beneficiary or other interested party;
- any other document that is relevant in your matter (such as if you have received a personal injury claim, inheritance, gift from parents, loans, redundancy payments, etc. during the relationship – the documents that show what you received and what happened to it).

This is not a complete list of everything that you need to disclose, and you should seek advice from your family lawyer about what is relevant in your matter.

When you file your application, you must also complete and file a: **Genuine Steps Certificate** confirming that you have complied with the pre-action procedures, taken genuine steps to resolve the matter or otherwise set out your reasons for seeking to be exempt from that requirement.

Preparing your application

When you are ready to lodge your application with the court, you will need to prepare the following documents:

- application;
- affidavit;

- financial statement, if your matter relates to property or maintenance;
- mediation certificate or exemption, if your matter relates to parenting;
- notice of risk.

Let's have a closer look at each of these documents.

The **application** sets out the information about each of the parties – their names, dates of birth, addresses and other contact information. The application will also include details of any children under 18 years of age – even in property matters. The application will include or have attached to it additional pages that set out the orders you want the court to make; that is, what you say the outcome should be.

In a parenting application, this might mean that you include orders about where the children are to live and how decisions are to be made. In a property application, this will include what you say should happen to the property that you have.

You will put in this document the orders that you would like the court to make for the short term (**interim orders**) and orders that you would like the court to make at the end of your matter (**final orders**). Sometimes these are the same.

Your **affidavit** is your statement of evidence. This document sets out what you say the history of your relationship has been, and any evidence that you have to support that. For example, evidence in a property might be that in 2005 you received a redundancy payment of $125,000. Your affidavit would set out how that happened and then you would attach a document that shows the amount you received, when you received it, from where you received it and what happened to it. In a parenting matter, evidence might be that your 8-year-old daughter Jessica has been diagnosed with Autism Spectrum Disorder.

Your affidavit would set out the information about Jessica's disorder and you might attach a report and diagnosis from a specialist.

The court rules require that if your matter is listed for an interim hearing (we'll talk more about that shortly), your affidavit must be no more than 10 pages with no more than 5 exhibits. This will allow the judge hearing your matter to review the relevant issues that are disputed and make a decision about your matter.

A **financial statement** sets out your current financial circumstances. It covers:

- your employment;
- your average weekly income;
- your average weekly expenses;
- assets in your name;
- liabilities in your name;
- details of your superannuation.

If you are also seeking maintenance, you must break down your weekly expenditure into expenses for yourself and expenses for your children.

Your **mediation certificate** will be prepared by the family dispute resolution practitioner who facilitated or attempted to facilitate your mediation. If you do not have a certificate you'll need to lodge an **exemption form** called **Affidavit – Non-Filing of Family Dispute Resolution Certificate**.

A **notice of risk** is required to be lodged in all applications before the court. It is a tool to make the court aware of any risks in matters relating to child abuse or family violence. It also allows the court to quickly refer matters to child safety agencies.

Lodging your documents

Once you have prepared your application, you can lodge it in one of two ways. You can lodge your documents in person at the court registry closest to you, or as is more commonly the case in recent times, lodge the documents via the Commonwealth Courts Portal – the online courts lodgement system.

Here, you can also see upcoming court dates for your matter, and view and download documents that have already been lodged.

Whether your application is lodged in person or online, you will be allocated the first court date. This is usually within 1 to 2 months. Sometimes earlier dates come up, but this is rare.

Providing a copy of the application to the other party

Once you have lodged your documents with the court, you will need to provide a copy of the documents to the other party. This is called **service** – you will have first encountered this term in **Chapter 5** when considering an application for divorce.

If you have a family lawyer assisting you, and the other party has a family lawyer assisting them, both lawyers can agree (with their client's permission) to receive the documents by email or post. If the other party's lawyer does not have their client's permission to receive documents this way, your lawyer will need to arrange **personal service** – that is, the personal delivery of the documents on the other party.

The personal service is usually undertaken by a third party, either someone you know or someone whose job it is to serve documents. That third party goes to the other party's home or workplace and gives them the documents. When you start a new application, the documents must be personally served in this way, unless the lawyers agree as described above. If the party receiving the documents refuses to accept them, the service agent can place them on the ground at their feet and describe the documents they are handing over.

It is important to remember that when you are the applicant, you are unable to give the documents to the other party yourself. It must be done by a third party.

The other party's response

After the other party has received the court application, they have 14 days to prepare a response to your application. In preparing a response, the following documents are prepared:

- response;
- affidavit;
- financial statement (in a property matter);
- notice of risk.

The **response** sets out the orders the other party is seeking. As for your application, this document should set out both interim and final orders.

The affidavit, financial statement and notice of risk are the same forms as covered earlier.

TRIAGE AND ASSESSMENT

When an application has been filed, the parties will be invited to complete an online risk screen. This allows the court to consider immediate safety risks, service referrals and appropriate case management. The matter may be allocated to a special list depending on the circumstances.

The Evatt List

The Evatt List is a specialist list for high-risk cases that provides support, resources and safeguards against those high-risk factors in family law matters. High-risk factors include:

- serious abuse or risk of abuse of a child whether physical, psychological or neglect;
- serious family violence or risk of serious family violence;
- a party's or a child's exposure to family violence or risk of being exposed to family violence;
- serious drug, alcohol and substances misuse that has caused harm to a child or a party;
- a party's mental health issues that have caused harm or risk of harm to a child or party;
- a party who poses a potential risk of self-harm;
- recent threats or attempts to abduct a child; or
- recent threats to harm a child or another person such as a new partner:

Critical Incident List

This specialist list was established in June 2022 for applications that are filed in circumstances where there is no parent available to care for a child or children as a result of death (including homicide), critical injury, or incarceration relating to family violence, and orders are sought to make appropriate arrangements for parental responsibility.

Magellan List

This is a discrete case management pathway for matters involving allegations of sexual abuse or serious physical abuse of children. Such matters can also include serious or escalating family violence resulting in serious psychological harm.

Indigenous List

This list differs from other court lists in that it makes the proceedings less formal, there are specialist support services available and the judge may decide to close the courtroom to the public. The intention in providing this list is to deliver equitable outcomes for Aboriginal and Torres Strait Islander communities and families.

National COVID-19 List

This is a specialist court list that deals with urgent family law disputes that have arisen from the COVID-19 pandemic. Issues in this list include parenting arrangements impacted by the pandemic, border restrictions, medical needs, travel, urgent or priority financial and maintenance matters, and other issues relating to the COVID-19 pandemic.

Property Lists

There are two specialised property lists – a **Priority Property Pools under $500,000 pilot list** and a **Major Complex Financial Proceedings List**.

There is also the **National Arbitration List** for those seeking to engage in Arbitration as an alternative to a judge-based decision to resolve their matter. Where parties elect to enter into that process (the parties must elect; it can only be ordered by agreement) the National Arbitration Judge will manage the process with a view to having the matter finalised by arbitration within 4 to 6 months of entering the list.

National Contravention List

This list commenced with the merged Court system on 1 September 2021. The intention of the national approach is to deal efficiently with all Contravention Applications. The application, once lodged, is reviewed by a Deputy Registrar and filed within 14 days (if accepted).

A first court date is allocated within 14 days of filing. On the first court date, directions are made for the hearing of the matter. The matter is allocated before a Senior Judicial Registrar or a Judge usually within 28 days of that first Court date.

At the point of filing and on the first court date, the application is triaged, which ensures that only properly prepared applications proceed before the Court. The 2021–22 Annual Report noted that in the 10 months since the commencement of the list, of the 1,605 applications filed, only 772 were accepted by the Deputy Registrar; the balance was rejected or requisitioned because the application was deficient or did not comply with the court rules.

THE NEW COURT PATHWAY

With the introduction of the merged Courts and the Central Practice Direction, the way in which matters are managed has been streamlined. It is intended to have each matter before the Court for a final hearing within 12 months of filing, with the outcome (judgement) handed down by the Judge after a contested hearing within 3 months of the hearing.

The Central Practice Direction sets out 10 core principles that underpin the exercise of the family law court and requires all steps taken in proceedings to follow those principles. Those principles are:

1. to prioritise the safety of children, vulnerable parties and litigants, issues of risk, including allegations of family violence.
2. to ensure that disputes are resolved according to law and as quickly, inexpensively and efficiently as possible.
3. to ensure the efficient and effective use of court and other resources while ensuring the appropriate handling of risks.

4. to triage matters through the court system prioritising internal and external dispute resolution processes.

5. to identify the appropriate time and manner in which to resolve disputes either by agreement or court order.

6. to manage non-compliance with court orders and processes effectively and early, including referring applications to a Judge, dismissing applications, proceeding on an undefended basis (where the Court will not hear from the defaulting party), and costs implications, including making orders that the defaulting party pay the other party's costs or where the lawyer is at fault an order that costs are paid by legal representatives.

7. to ensure that parties and their lawyers take a sensible and prag-matic approach to litigation and only incur such costs as are fair, reasonable and proportionate to the issues that are genuinely in dispute.

8. to make full disclosure to assist the court, negotiate, and come to an agreement about the issues to be determined by the Court.

9. to ensure that parties and legal representatives are familiar with the issues in the case and fully prepared for all court events.

10. to make sure that matters move through the system as quickly and fairly as possible, with judgments being delivered as soon as possible after the receipt of final submissions.

The simplified pathway includes the following events.

First Court Event

The First Court Event with a Judicial Registrar usually occurs within 1 to 2 months of filing. This is a procedural hearing to work out:

- the type of matter – property or parenting;
- what is in dispute (for example, a request for an increase in time with the children, or a request that the other party disclose documents and attend mediation);
- the lawyers involved in the matter;
- whether agreement can be reached about some or all of the issues in dispute;
- whether there is agreement about how your matter will move forward.

If your lawyer and the other party's lawyer are able to agree on the best direction to take your matter, or if you and the other party are able to agree on parts (if not all) of your matter, this is the better way to progress the matter on the day.

If there are other issues that require a hearing in the meantime, the Judicial Registrar will refer the matter for an **interim hearing** (described in the next section) on a separate day.

If you reach agreement, the court can make these orders as consent orders.

It is important to remember that while a Judicial Registrar can determine limited issues (such as who will prepare a family report or valuation), they do not have the power to determine substantive issues in dispute.

Interim hearing

If the Judicial Registrar allocates an interim hearing, you will be allocated a set time to put forward your arguments and try to convince a Senior Judicial Registrar that your orders are the better orders in the circumstances.

In an interim hearing, ordinarily you do not have to give evidence in the witness box – though it's important to know this depends on the matter in dispute and the evidence in your affidavit. Usually an interim hearing is an application **on the papers** – that is, that the Senior Judicial Registrar will read your application and affidavit, and listen to **submissions** (arguments) from you or your lawyer about why your outcome is the preferred outcome.

You will usually receive the decision of the interim hearing on the day or within a couple of weeks; again, though, this depends on the Senior Judicial Registrar and the matter to be decided.

Mediation

You can reach agreement about going to mediation before your proceedings start or during your proceedings. Sometimes the Court will order that you attend mediation with an independent mediator who will assist you and the other party to try to resolve your matter. There is more information about mediation in **Chapter 7**.

Court Dispute Resolution Process

The 2021 amendments introduced Court-facilitated Dispute Resolution Process (Court DRP). This process is similar to the Conciliation Conference which has previously been available for financial matters but the Court DRP is for parenting matters only. The process is facilitated by a Judicial Registrar and the event is compulsory for parties to attend where it is a formal court event.

When the Court makes an order for a Court DRP, specific orders are made for the case management of that process as follows:

- each party must prepare a case outline setting out the issues in dispute and orders they are seeking. This must be exchanged with the other parties and the Court 7 days prior to the scheduled Court DRP.

- 2 to 3 days prior to the formal Court DRP there is an intake session (part 1). This is a conversation by telephone with the Judicial Registrar who is facilitating the process to check in with the parties about the process and obtain a brief understanding of any issues.
- The Court DRP (part 2) is the mediation process itself. This is a confidential process where the parties try to resolve all issues before the Court. The Judicial Registrar goes between the parties to assist in the negotiation.
- If an agreement is reached, the Judicial Registrar will make the orders to conclude the matter on a final basis, if all issues are resolved, or on an interim basis if some or most of the issues are resolved.

The Court has the option to include a Court Children's Expert in the process. A Court Children's Expert is a family consultant (usually a social worker or psychologist) who works at the Court and can assist the parties to consider the matter from the children's perspective and help parents maintain their focus on those perspectives.

Conciliation conference

In a property matter, if the combined value of the parties' property is modest (say $200,000–300,000) and you and/or the other party do not have the financial means to attend private mediation, you can ask the court for a conciliation conference. This is a **dispute resolution event** for a property matter. This conference only occurs with the court's permission, as it is a process organised and funded by the court.

A conciliation conference is a property mediation with a Judicial

Registrar of the court. Conferences are allocated either a half day or full day on the day. A Judicial Registrar will review the matter and assist the parties in trying to resolve their dispute. If agreement is reached, the registrar can make consent orders. If agreement cannot be reached, the matter is referred back to the case management Judicial Registrar.

The dispute resolution event, whether for property or parenting, must happen within 5 months of the filing date of the application.

Family report

If your matter involves parenting arrangements, you might seek an order that everyone attends for a family report process. The judge might also review your matter and decide that a family report would help in resolving your matter. There is more information about what is involved in a family report in the parenting section in **Chapter 3**.

Directions/mentions

After your Interim Hearing or Dispute Resolution Event your matter will return to the case management Judicial Registrar for mention. This type of court event is procedural – that is, you go to the court to check in about how your matter is progressing: have you had mediation, has the family report been released, and has disclosure been completed? It is not an opportunity to argue about interim matters such as asking for more time for the children to spend with you or the other party, or whether there should be a change to the interim financial arrangements.

Compliance and Readiness Hearing

After you have tried all possible avenues to resolve your matter through mediation, negotiation, etc. (see **Chapter 7**), if it is clear that your matter needs to be determined by a judge, your matter will be listed for a Compliance and Readiness Hearing. This should occur within

6 months of the date of filing your application. This is a court day allocated to all matters awaiting a trial date. There are usually 20 to 30 matters listed on the day, all seeking trial dates.

Before the Compliance and Readiness Hearing, you will have prepared a summary of your trial and the issues that are still in dispute. If you fail to do this, the judge can refuse to allocate a trial date and you go to the end of the queue of matters awaiting a hearing. You must also file an Undertaking as to Disclosure confirming you have disclosed all relevant documents and a Certificate of Readiness confirming the matter is ready for hearing.

Your final hearing should be listed within 12 months from the date your application was filed. At the time of publication of this edition, the wait time for a trial date in the Brisbane Registry is between 7 and 10 months from the Compliance and Readiness Hearing.

TRIAL

You have waited for your trial date for some time, and the day is finally upon you. In the lead-up to your trial, you will have prepared, either by yourself or with the assistance of your family lawyer, updated affidavits of any evidence you want the court to consider. You will have submitted a schedule of the orders you want the court to make.

When you turn up to court, more than likely you will find that yours is not the only matter listed for final hearing that day. The courts usually list two to three matters per day on a trial day in case one matter settles; then the other can proceed. However, if two out of three matters are proceeding, the third matter is going to miss out that day.

If your matter proceeds, the following key terms will be relevant for you:

You will likely have a **barrister** assisting your family lawyer. A barrister is a lawyer who has undertaken additional studies and training, and is skilled in litigation and evidence. They will assist your family lawyer to run your hearing. They will argue your case before the judge and ask questions of witnesses in the case. If your matter is going to a final hearing, you will want to ensure that you have a barrister to assist you.

Evidence in chief is a legal term that refers to your affidavit material. You do not need to get in the witness box and tell your whole story, as you will have prepared an affidavit, which sets out your evidence about your matter. At a trial, this is called your evidence in chief.

When you give evidence you will be **cross-examined**. This means that the barrister or lawyer for the other party will ask you questions about your evidence. The purpose of these questions is to test your evidence and to put the other party's case to you and see whether you agree or accept that what the other party says is true. It gets a bit complicated, which is why you have a barrister and a lawyer. Your family lawyer should make sure you are prepared for this process in the lead-up to your hearing.

The process of being cross-examined is not a pleasant experience. It is very stressful and distressing to sit in a witness box before the judge being asked questions by a person whose role it is to discredit you to prove the other side's case. Quite often, regardless of all the preparation done, you will forget the advice given to you by your lawyers. For that reason, it is so very important to invest your time in making sure you are prepared for that process.

At the end of the trial, **submissions** are made to the judge to summarise the evidence and the key points for each party's case.

The judge will then **reserve their decision**, which means that they will go away, think about all the evidence they've heard and make a decision about the matter.

Waiting

Judges will endeavour to let the parties know their decision within 3 months of the hearing date. Unfortunately, this rarely occurs given the demands on a judge's time, with parties waiting 6, 12 or even 18 months before receiving a judgment. During this time there is nothing that the parties can do except wait.

There are protocols in place for judgments to be followed up if it has been a long time, and your family lawyer can talk to you more about that if this applies to you. The 2021–22 annual report released by the Federal Circuit and Family Court of Australia shows that the largest number of complaints made to the courts are about the delay in receiving a judgment.

Judgment

When the judge is ready, you will be notified that they're going to deliver their judgment. Usually, you will receive a few days' notice of the judgment. I recall one matter where, having waited for 11 months for the decision, we were notified that the judgment was being delivered at the same time it was received by email. On other occasions, I have received between 2 and 4 days' notice. It will always depend on the judge.

The judgment will be delivered in one of two ways.

The judge can deliver an **oral judgment**. This means that the judge reads out the decision, the evidence that was considered and which decision is the right decision.

Alternatively, the judgment will be **in writing**. If this is the case, the judge will read out the orders they are making and otherwise give the parties (**publish**) a copy of the written decision and reasons for it.

Appeal

All decisions are subject to the right of a party to **appeal** the decision. You can't file an appeal of the decision simply because you don't agree with it. You must assert that the judge made an error; that is, that the judge got something wrong either in the evidence they reviewed or considered, or that they applied the law incorrectly. An appeal must be lodged within 28 days of the decision.

TIMEFRAMES

So when you pull this entire process through a timeframe, what does it look like? The answer, most commonly, is a bit like 'Well, how long is a piece of string?' The length of time it takes for your matter to progress from application to final hearing will depend on the type of matter, the judge hearing the matter, any number of complications that pop up along the way, how the parties progress the matter, and the like.

Historically, the process from application to final hearing (in cases where resolution isn't reached along the way) can take between 2 and 4 years. Under the new Central Practice Direction, the courts endeavour to have matters concluded within 12 months. However, in contested matters, this rarely happens. As the older 'legacy' matters are cleared from the system, matters may start to be resolved more quickly, provided there are enough judges and resources to support them.

STAYING OUT OF COURT, OR GETTING OUT QUICKLY

With all this in mind, you can see why you might want to avoid the system. The reality is that some matters need a court determination. Some parties won't comply with reasonable requests and need the forceful prod of the court. Other matters relate to serious allegations of abuse, which are not going to resolve by other means. Generally, however, if you can avoid going to court, you should do everything in your power to do that.

In the next chapter we'll consider alternative ways to resolve your matter. We'll look at the other methods of dispute resolution available to you and, when you reach agreement, ways in which you can document your matter.

Once you are in the court system, can you get out?

At any time along the way, you can try to resolve your matter. Most of the time, matters will be settled or resolved before they need a final hearing. The odds of your matter being resolved before a final hearing are high. In the Family Court of Australia, only 15% of matters go to final hearing and of those, 65% are resolved on the day of hearing without a judge needing to hear the matter. Mediation has a 95% success rate. There are ways to get off the rollercoaster and get on with your life.

Chapter 7:

Alternative ways to resolve your matter

Having read about why you would want to avoid the court system, what are your alternatives? There are a range of different ways that you can work towards resolving your family law matter. There are different types of documents that you can prepare yourself or with the assistance of a lawyer to finalise your matter without the need to go to court.

This chapter is divided into two sections. The first section looks at the practical steps you can take to resolve your matter without going to court, and different types of dispute resolution you can undertake. The second section looks at documenting any agreement you reach, where appropriate, to make sure that it is a binding document that finalises your matter.

PRACTICAL WAYS TO RESOLVE YOUR MATTER

Family dispute resolution

Family dispute resolution (FDR) is a formal process that facilitates a discussion between parties who have separated to work towards resolving their parenting or property dispute. FDR is a service provided by organisations such as Family Relationship Centres, Relationships Australia and Legal Aid (in each state), along with other community organisations. FDR can also be facilitated by lawyers, social workers, psychologists and other practitioners who specialise in mediation.

It is important to note, particularly for parenting matters, that only registered family dispute resolution facilitators can issue a certificate that indicates you have made a genuine attempt to resolve your matter (as required by the *Family Law Act* if you need to commence proceedings for your parenting matter).

The *Family Law Act* makes family dispute resolution compulsory in parenting matters if your matter will ultimately end up before the court.

That is, you must make a genuine attempt to resolve your parenting matter before filing an application seeking parenting orders. There are exemptions to attending compulsory family dispute resolution; for example, if you have reached agreement and are lodging consent orders (see 'Consent orders' later in this chapter); there are allegations of child abuse, neglect or family violence; or other urgent circumstances. You should consult a family lawyer if you think these exemptions might apply to you.

What is the process for FDR?

Each organisation will have a different FDR process depending on whether you are using a government, community or private service. A government-funded or community service will usually provide an intake service that is followed by a group or information session, and then followed by the FDR session. The FDR session will involve the parties to the dispute and the facilitator. On some occasions you can include a support person, but all parties including the other party and facilitator must agree to this process. Lawyers are usually not involved if the process is facilitated through a government or community service.

The type of service chosen will depend largely on the financial circumstances of the parties. Those with children tend to contact services such as Relationships Australia, Centacare or the Family Relationships Centres directly. They will not be able to choose their FDR practitioner; one will be allocated to them from the centre they attend.

During the FDR session, the FDR practitioner must let you know about certain aspects of the session. The process is confidential, and discussions are held without prejudice . This means that what you or the other party say, admit or concede during the session is confidential and can't be used later against the person making the concession if your matter ends up in court. The only time confidentiality does not apply is if threats are made against a person or property, if the practitioner considers that a child is at risk, or a crime has been or may be committed.

The FDR practitioner will also give you information about the service provided, their qualifications, how to provide feedback or complaints about the service and ways that you can resolve your matter through parenting plans.

It is important to note that the FDR practitioner is impartial and independent. They are not there to take sides. They are not there to make the decision for you or provide you with legal advice about your rights or the process generally. Their role is to help you to objectively explore options to resolve your matter.

If you reach agreement, any document that you and your partner sign as a result of the FDR session will be known as a **parenting plan**. A parenting plan is not a binding document and, depending on your circumstances, you should seek advice from a lawyer about converting your parenting plan into a legally binding consent order.

If your agreement includes property settlement, the document will be known as a **heads of agreement**. It is not a binding agreement and you will need to document the agreement reached by way of a consent order or financial agreement as set out in the second section of this chapter.

If you were unable to resolve your matter, the FDR practitioner will issue a certificate stating that you attended an FDR session and made a genuine attempt to resolve your matter. You can then seek further advice from a lawyer about whether court proceedings are necessary.

Family Relationship Centres provide a free FDR process to those clients who earn less than $50,000 or are in receipt of Commonwealth health and social security benefits. If only one parent's income is less than $50,000, the other parent may have to make a financial contribution to the FDR costs.

Child-inclusive processes for parenting matters

Some FDR centres offer a **child-inclusive process** that runs alongside the FDR process. This doesn't mean that the child participates in the FDR process itself; rather, a child consultant, usually a practitioner with psychology or social work training, will meet with the child separately to the FDR process to give the child an opportunity to tell their story and express their views about what has been happening. The child consultant will then report the outcomes of that session to the parents in a joint session so that both parents are hearing the feedback at the same time. From here, the parents can consider the thoughts and views of the children when working to resolve their matter.

The purpose of child inclusive processes is to allow the parents to keep the children at the forefront of their minds when they are having discussions with each other about the future arrangements for the children.

Child-inclusive processes are not suitable for all families and the FDR practitioner will consider and assess whether it is appropriate. In my experience, the process can be quite confronting for parents, particularly where they are unaware of the impact their behaviours (no matter how much they try to 'act normally') are having on their children. I recall one particular meeting that was quite harrowing for the lawyers and clients involved, where the child psychologist explained to the parents the children's experiences of separation. I have also seen parents try to use this process for their own advantage, thinking that if the children have their say, the parent would get the parenting orders they wanted. Often, in this kind of scenario, not everything goes to plan for those parents because during separation children will commonly be trying to please both parents, desperately wanting to keep their family together. A child's wish to spend more time with one parent is likely to have been voiced to the other parent as well.

Like the FDR process generally, the feedback and views obtained from the children during the child-inclusive process are confidential and cannot be used later by a parent during court proceedings.

Mediation

Mediation is similar to the FDR process and can also be used to resolve both property and parenting matters. Most mediations are facilitated by private practitioners such as lawyers, social workers, barristers and other trained and accredited mediators. Some mediators are not FDR practitioners. This is important to note in parenting disputes – if you are a party to a parenting dispute, only an FDR practitioner can issue the required family law certificate that indicates you made a genuine attempt to resolve your matter. If you think your parenting matter is one that might end up in court, make sure that your mediator is also a registered FDR practitioner.

You can locate a mediator through AIFLAM, which is the national body for family law arbitrators and mediators, at http://www.aiflam.org.au; alternatively, or you can contact the local law association or barristers' association in your state. You should make sure that your mediator has national accreditation and complies with the Australian National Mediator Standards.

What is the process for mediation?

Most private mediations are run in a similar way to FDR. The mediator will usually arrange for an intake session where they speak with you about the issues you are concerned about. This is a one-on-one session with just the mediator and you. It is a confidential session so that the mediator can get an understanding of the most important issues for you. Following the intake session – sometimes on the same day, sometimes on different days – the mediation will commence. The mediator will let you know those same things that are relevant to the FDR process – that is, that the mediation is confidential and without prejudice, and that confidentiality is only waived if threats are made against a person or property, if the practitioner considers that a child is at risk, or a crime has been or will be committed.

The same rules about support persons apply; however, in private mediation you can have a lawyer present.

There are some advantages to having a lawyer present during these discussions, and for that reason some will prefer the mediation process to the FDR process. A lawyer will be able to advise you about your rights and provide other options to resolve your matter. Remember that a mediator or FDR practitioner is impartial and can't provide you with advice about your rights. A lawyer might also bring documents with them that can more readily be made into a binding agreement.

A mediation will usually commence with an information session about how the mediation works and what happens if you can't resolve your matter. There may then be a session that involves only the lawyers to iron out any details like the property pool or any contentious issues that the mediator feels may impede the negotiations. Most mediations then proceed on a shuttle basis – that is, with the meditator moving between the rooms to see if an agreement can be reached.

Negotiation directly or through lawyers

Depending on the scope of the dispute and the personalities of the parties, some property or parenting matters can be resolved through negotiation between lawyers.

Negotiation is beneficial when the **scope of the dispute** (the differences between each party's position) is limited or, for example, where the parties are not comfortable to engage directly with the other party through mediation or in-person discussions. It can also be beneficial to clients who have experienced domestic and family violence or power imbalance, because this process is safer for them.

What is the process for negotiation?
Negotiation can include conversations by telephone or in person, exchanging letters and emails, and providing documents. The lawyers then engage with their clients in person, by correspondence or phone to discuss offers that have been exchanged.

If you have engaged a lawyer, chances are you are going through a negotiation process without even realising it. As they exchange offers in their correspondence, lawyers will gradually reduce the number of issues that are disputed and work towards resolving the matter.

Arbitration

Arbitration is a process where the parties choose a private arbitrator to decide how their property is to be divided, or whether spousal or de facto partner maintenance is payable. An arbitrator must be a legal practitioner who is experienced in family law matters either through accreditation or years of experience, and who has completed specialist arbitration training. The arbitrator must apply the principles set out in the *Family Law Act 1975*, as the court would do.

One of the benefits of arbitration over a court process is that the parties to the dispute ultimately control and determine the process for resolving their dispute. Another advantage is that arbitration is efficient and quick, private and confidential, final and enforceable and conducted applying legal principles.

As for a mediator, you can locate an arbitrator through AIFLAM, which is the national body for family law arbitrators and mediators http://www.aiflam.org.au. Alternatively, you can contact the local law association or barristers' association in your state.

What is the process for arbitration?

Parties can have the matter determined either **on the papers**, where relevant documents, evidence and submissions are lodged and the arbitrator makes a determination of the issues, whether through a **simple arbitration** involving some level of hearing, evidence and cross-examination or a **complex arbitration** similar to court proceedings.

After the hearing, the arbitrator will hand down their decision. The decision is called an **award**. The award must be in writing and set out the reasons for the decision and any facts relied upon in determining the matter. Either party can then register the award with the court. The award is enforceable as if it was an order of the court. Awards are also subject to a review by a judicial officer on questions of law only, in the event either party takes issue with the award.

With the significant delays in the family law courts, many parties are turning to arbitration to resolve their matter. Arbitration is cost-effective and allows parties to resolve their matter far sooner than through the family law courts.

Collaborative law

Collaborative law is the practice of working co-operatively with your former spouse to resolve your matter, with the mutual agreement of your spouse not to go to court. In addition to specifically trained collaborative lawyers, other professionals such as accountants, financial advisors, mediators and psychologists can be engaged to guide the parties to a settlement arrangement that benefits the family as a whole, despite the separation that has occurred.

The focus of collaborative practice is to minimise the conflict between the parties and reach a settlement by adopting problem-solving methods.

A family lawyer who is experienced in collaborative law matters will be able to assess whether your matter is suitable for collaborative law.

What is the process for collaborative law?

To further each party's commitment not to go to court, the parties and their lawyers execute a contract stating that the lawyers will withdraw from representing their client if the matter cannot be resolved without commencing court proceedings.

This does not prevent the parties from going to court as a last resort, but changes the dynamics of negotiation and focuses the parties on a swift, cost-effective, interests-based resolution as opposed to position-based litigation.

A good visual example of how collaborative law works is to think about two children fighting over an orange. To end the dispute, the parent cuts the orange in half (position based with each child having half). Both children remain distressed. It turns out that one child was only after the juice of the orange, whereas the other wanted the peel for an experiment (interests based with each parent wanting a particular part of the orange for their own interest).

Thinking then about family law matters, this analogy shows the focus in the collaborative law approach is working out what each party is hoping to achieve. One party may want to keep the house for a sense of security and isn't so concerned about whether it is the right percentage of assets. In another matter, one party might just be happy ensuring they keep all their superannuation as they are thinking about the future. It will always depend on what each individual person hopes to achieve from their family law settlement.

As this section sets out, there are different ways you can work towards resolving your matter. Filing your application in court should be seen as the last resort only.

In the next section, you will find information about the types of agreements you can create – whether by yourself, with the other party or with the assistance of your lawyer – to record any agreement reached.

DOCUMENTING YOUR AGREEMENT

Property matters

When you reach agreement about how your property will be distributed after separation, it is essential to document the agreement in a formal way.

Without a formal agreement – that is, either a financial agreement entered into under the *Family Law Act* or a consent order made by the Federal Circuit and Family Court of Australia – there is no certainty that your matter is truly at an end.

You will also need a formal agreement if you are transferring property between spouses and want to avoid paying transfer duty on the transfer of property. Formally documenting your property agreement by way of a consent order or financial agreement allows you an exemption on transfer duty ordinarily payable on the transfer of property. For example, if you have agreed that one of you will retain a property that is owned jointly, without a financial agreement you will need to pay transfer duty on one-half of the value of the property. With a financial agreement or consent order, no transfer duty is payable.

From speaking with my clients, I have learned that the biggest concerns people have in formally documenting their property settlement are:

- They have reached an agreement and simply want to finalise the matter without fuss;

- They are worried that going to see a lawyer will delay and complicate their matter where they have already reached an agreement;
- They are concerned about the costs in preparing a detailed agreement when they are sure their matter is straightforward.

Far too often, I have seen a scenario where the parties have written down their agreement on a piece of paper and gone to the effort of signing it in the presence of a Justice of the Peace, only for the agreement to be ignored when one party seeks a further distribution of property. A written agreement, signed in the presence of the Justice of the Peace or other witness, is not a binding document unless it is a consent order or financial agreement.

Consent orders

Where you have reached agreement about your property matter, you can make an application to the Federal Circuit and Family Court of Australia to have the agreement made into a formal court order. In essence, a consent order is an order that both parties agree or consent to the court making.

What is the process for a consent order?

The process involves completing an **application for consent orders** and preparing formal court orders (**proposed orders**) in the form that will be accepted by the court. The parties sign the application and proposed orders and lodge them with the Court, paying the required lodgement fee.

This can be done with or without legal advice, though I recommend seeking advice about the proposed orders to make sure they are within the range of percentages that the court would find acceptable to make the orders. It is also important to consult a lawyer about the drafting of your proposed orders. I have assisted many clients who have lodged orders with the court only to have them requisitioned because the court took issue with the wording of the orders.

You can enter into a consent order about all aspects of property settlement except spouse maintenance obligation, which you cannot contract out of. Any reference to spouse maintenance is best dealt with in a financial agreement.

Financial agreement

A financial agreement is an alternative way to formalise your property settlement. It can include all of the same information and agreement (similar to the proposed orders) that you have reached. The difference lies in the strict legal obligations imposed by the *Family Law Act*. These exist because through a financial agreement, you are contracting out of your right to have the Court determine your property matter, including any right to spouse maintenance.

For a financial agreement to be binding, the following conditions must be met:

- it must be in writing;
- it must be signed by all parties;
- before signing the agreement, each party must receive independent legal advice from a legal practitioner about the effects of the agreement on the rights of the party, and about the advantages and disadvantages of entering into the agreement at the time the advice is provided;
- before or after signing the agreement, each party must receive a signed statement by the legal practitioner confirming that the above advice was provided with a copy of the statement given

to the other party or their lawyer;

- the agreement has not been terminated by further agreement or set aside by the court.

Due to the nature of a financial agreement, where parties are opting out of using the family law system to resolve their matter, a significant amount of work goes into the preparation of the agreement to make sure that it complies with the strict legal requirements and that it is binding and protects your interests.

For those reasons, a financial agreement differs from a consent order. Both parties must engage with and see a lawyer for advice about the financial agreement.

How to streamline the document process

If you have reached an amicable agreement with your spouse about how to divide your property and need assistance in preparing the documents to finalise your matter, here are my tips to help you streamline the process.

Prepare a detailed schedule of the property that you own either jointly or in individual names.

Preparing a detailed schedule of all property owned assists your lawyer in putting together the agreement. You must include *all* property. In this context, property includes assets, liabilities and superannuation. For example, your schedule might include real property, shares, investments, cars, bikes, boats, cash in the bank, a mortgage, a line of credit, a credit card, other personal loans, or superannuation. Your schedule will include property whether in joint names or individual names, regardless of whether you had the property before, during or after your relationship.

With regard to your furniture – unless you have antique items, grand pianos, artwork or other furniture of significant value – it is not necessary to list every single item of furniture that you own. You should be able to agree that your furniture has a certain value. This will not be the insured value – it will be the value you might get if you had to sell your furniture.

Collate documents that confirm the values of the property included in your schedule.

In all property matters, regardless of whether you are at the height of negotiations or have amicably reached a settlement, each party has an obligation to disclose all relevant documents that support their property matter. When you have reached an agreement, it is particularly important to disclose the following documents:

- valuations you have obtained for any real property; or, if you haven't had the properties formally valued, a market appraisal that considers comparable sales;
- current superannuation valuations;
- investment portfolio summaries;
- bank statements showing current balances for all accounts held;
- valuations for any vehicles – you can obtain an estimate from redbook.com.au;
- valuations of any business interests;
- any other document that supports a value you have included on your property schedule.

Write down the details of your agreement.

You should make specific notes about your agreement. These notes might include comments such as: Sue will receive the Camp Hill property; Bill will receive the Noosa property. Sue will pay to Bill $100,000, being half of the difference in the equity of the two properties. Bill will keep his shares. Sue and Bill will each keep their own superannuation. Sue will collect the piano, dining table and spare TV from the Noosa property within 14 days. And so on.

Setting out your agreement in this way makes it straightforward for your lawyer to then draft the agreement for you.

Make notes about the contributions you have each made to the relationship.
Whether you are entering into a financial agreement or preparing an application for consent orders, your lawyer needs to know about how you acquired the property that you have. You need to think about:

- what property you had at the beginning of your relationship;
- whether you received any special contributions during the relationship – such as an inheritance from an estate, or a personal injury claim – and make notes about where the funds came from and what you did with them;
- any special arrangements that have been in place since separation;
- the income of each of you;
- if you have children, what the arrangements for them were during the relationship and what they are now.

This information is important because it allows your lawyer to draft either the financial agreement or the application for consent orders, and particularly for the financial agreement, provide you with advice as required by the *Family Law Act*.

Remember that the lawyer who prepares your agreement can only act for one party.

Even though you have reached an agreement and you both have a common goal as to what you want to achieve, a lawyer can only act for one party. This is because the lawyer's role is broader than simply preparing the agreement. Whether the lawyer is preparing a financial agreement or consent orders, they have obligations to provide you with advice and ensure that the agreement is drafted appropriately in accordance with your instructions. The rights and interests of one party may differ from the rights and interests of the other. In those circumstances, to act for both parties would give rise to a conflict of interests.

Regardless of whether your property settlement is amicable, each party to an agreement is entitled to and should seek their own independent legal advice about the agreement.

You should determine between you which party will instruct a lawyer to prepare the agreement. That party should then see a lawyer armed with all of the information referred to above.

Two final points

In reaching an agreement about your property settlement, there are two final points that you need to be aware of and talk with your lawyer about.

Firstly, entering into consent orders only does not finalise any spouse maintenance issues. What this means is that you can finalise your property settlement, but then up to 1 year after your divorce has become finalised or 2 years after you separate from your de facto relationship, a party can still bring an application for spouse maintenance.

Secondly, if you reach an agreement about sharing superannuation and seek an order that superannuation be split, there are some extra steps involved. You need to seek the consent of your superannuation fund's trustee before you sign any orders, which may add to the time taken to finalise your matter. If these matters are relevant to you, you should speak further with your lawyer.

Agreements about your parenting arrangements

The law encourages parents to reach an agreement about how to parent their children after separation, and to regard the court system as a last resort. This is not only because court proceedings can be time-consuming and expensive, but also because co-operation between separated parents will reduce stress for children and parents alike.

Parenting plans

A parenting plan is a less formal way of documenting your parenting arrangements with the other parent than an agreement. This can be a good way of recording the arrangements if you and the other parent are able to co-operate and do not want or need to enter into a legally enforceable agreement.

A parenting plan can provide details of where your children live, how they will spend time with each of the parents, how parents will exercise their responsibility and how to resolve any disagreements that may arise, as well as any other arrangement that relates to the parenting of the children.

Parenting plans are not legally enforceable and cannot be registered in court. If you wish to register your parenting arrangement with the court, you should consider a consent order.

While a parenting plan is not enforceable, if there is a dispute in court later on, the court may look to the terms of any existing parenting plan to determine what may be in the best interests of the child.

Also, if you have a pre-existing parenting order (made either by an agreement or by a judge) you can, at any time, override that arrangement by entering into a parenting plan with the other parent. Similarly, an existing parenting plan can be overridden by a new parenting plan, consent order or parenting order.

> Take Alexis and Mary, who have two children aged 6 and 8. About three years ago they had orders made after their court hearing that set out the time the children were to spend with each parent. Recently Mary started a new job, which means it is difficult for her to be available for the children after school. Alexis works early mornings and can be available after school. Alexis and Mary attend mediation and reach agreement about the changes to their parenting arrangements. Most of the clauses of their parenting order are still okay, so they simply agree in a parenting plan on the limited changes to the weekly living arrangements.

You are able to alter your previous parenting plan by agreement with the other parent or by creating a new plan to replace it.

Parenting plan requirements
Both parents must enter into the parenting plan willingly, without either parent coercing or threatening the other in any way. The plan must be in writing, signed and dated by both parents. Both parents should keep a copy.

While parenting plans are usually formed between the child's parents, they can also be made with other people, such as between a parent and step-parent, or between parents and grandparents.

Consent orders

As with any agreement reached for your property settlement, you can apply to the court for consent orders, which set out the orders you have agreed to for the care of your children. Consent orders are similar to a parenting plan, because they are also formed by both parents reaching an agreement about their parenting arrangements. Significantly, however, consent orders are made by the family law courts, are legally enforceable, and penalties may apply in circumstances where the orders are found to have been contravened by a party. You may prefer this type of arrangement if you want a legally enforceable agreement.

What is the process for a consent order?

Generally, a consent order for a parenting agreement is drafted by a family lawyer, signed by both parties (and their lawyers), then lodged with the court, together with any relevant documentation. If the order is approved by the court, it is binding and enforceable for both parents.

When considering whether to approve an application for a consent order, the court will look to whether the proposed order is in the child's best interests. The court will also consider the legal framework referred to here.

If your proposed order includes arrangements for the child to live with a non-parent, the court must be satisfied that it is appropriate to make such an order in the circumstances. The court will also require the parties to attend a conference with a family consultant prior to making the order.

You do not need to engage in the family dispute resolution process (outlined earlier in this chapter) to file an application for consent orders with the court, and you are able to apply for a consent order without having a current case before the court.

Now that we have considered the alternative ways to resolve your matter and the types of documents to record the agreement you have reached, we will look at how a family lawyer can assist you.

Chapter 8:

Choosing a lawyer and preparing for your first visit

HOW DO YOU CHOOSE THE RIGHT FAMILY LAWYER FOR YOU?

Going through a separation is a profoundly personal journey. As you have seen in the chapters before this and as we'll discuss in **Chapter 10,** no matter how strong you feel you are, you will go through ups and downs, good days and bad days – sometimes very bad days. The person you choose to guide you through the family law process is therefore a significant personal decision for you.

Over the years I have asked my clients what the important things are that they look for when they are choosing their family lawyer. Their responses vary, but key themes emerge; while some of these themes won't apply to everyone, they do offer some points to consider.

Before we flesh out those themes, meet Stephanie. Stephanie came to see me in a state of high stress and anxiety. She had been in a relationship for three years, had two very young children and was parenting her stepson full-time. The nature of Stephanie's relationship meant that when her ex-partner said 'jump', she asked 'how high'. She had lived a life of walking on eggshells and was reactive to every demand that came. On reflection, Stephanie says:

Before settling on my family lawyer, I had a meeting with another firm to discuss my legal issues. I came out of that meeting in tears, feeling very distressed and overwhelmed. My sister encouraged me to try again and to get a second opinion.

Within minutes of meeting with my family lawyer, I felt safe. I suppose that is a strange word to use. But it was like a security blanket that I could trust I was being looked after. I almost immediately felt a gentle and kind approach, but with a confidence and strength that just made me feel completely safe and supported. For the first time since my legal issues had arisen, I felt that someone was taking my burden off my shoulders and allowing me to breathe for a moment. I came out of that first meeting smiling for the first time in a long time.

Turning now to the key themes:

- A **personal referral** from a friend or other professional can be important. Through that referral you can understand that the lawyer has had an impact on the referrer such that they would gladly recommend their services. A professional referral could come from another lawyer or advisor and will generally be someone who has worked with the lawyer before. Lawyers stake a lot on their personal reputation and a personal referral is often the best endorsement a lawyer can have.

- The lawyer's **core values must be aligned with your values**. There are many different tried and tested styles of legal practice when it comes to the personal nature of family law. But you may not be looking for a robust, heavy-hitting lawyer who may lead you to victory at the cost of your relationships. Often greater success is had trying to work amicably or collaboratively, particularly where children are concerned. Michelle says, 'I was looking for a lawyer who could handle but not unduly provoke the personality of my ex.' Craig says, 'I wanted to feel secure that my lawyer could deal with the psychology of the other party.'

- **Trust and confidence** is crucial. It can only be established through meeting with your intended lawyer and developing a relationship based on the trust that they have the requisite experience to fully advise you in your circumstances and the confidence that they can progress you to a resolution. Michelle says 'the inability to make eye contact with me' was something that ruled out prior lawyers she had met with.

- The ability to provide a **sense of calm or solidarity** in a chaotic or complex environment is crucial. Your family lawyer should talk through all of your anxieties and concerns, and provide you with objective advice. This process has the ability to calm things down and assist clients with focusing on the big picture, rather than invoking the reactive nature of family law.
- Your lawyer needs to truly **understand how you function as a person** and how you will respond to certain things. It is important to find someone who can advise you without talking down to you or patronising you, as well as being able to talk things through rather than just telling you how it is. While your family lawyer can advise you on the law and the best approach to your matter, there must be give and take so that you can work together towards the goals you have set. Having a lawyer who can manage that and work with you as a team is enormously beneficial.

As you can see from this list, it might take one or two times to find the right fit, and that's okay. Just because you have been to see a family lawyer doesn't mean you are committed to that lawyer and are unable to change.

Regardless of what is important to you in selecting a family lawyer who is right for you, it's essential to prepare for your first appointment. It might be that you're unable to do this – that is, given the circumstances of your separation, you are not coping – and that's okay. It's enough that you have made the appointment and got yourself there. If you have the wherewithal, though, here are some tips to prepare for that first visit.

PREPARING FOR YOUR FIRST VISIT TO YOUR FAMILY LAWYER

In my years of practice, I have perceived a consistent pattern that those clients who take the time to think about what they want to achieve from their first meeting find the process more beneficial. While it is inevitable that some clients will not know where to start, usually because of the manner in which their relationship ended, most clients have the means to think through those things that are important to understand from this first meeting.

In particular, I have found that by giving some attention to the following points in preparation, you will get the most out of your first visit to your family lawyer.

Think about what property you have

Before seeking advice about a property settlement, it is helpful for both you, and your lawyer in turn, if you sit down and work out what property you have and the value you anticipate each item of property has.

Your property might include your home and investment properties (whether you own these properties yourself, with someone else, or as part of a company or family trust). It might include vehicles, money in the bank, shares and other investments, the contents in your home, and any companies or family trust structures. Property also includes any debt attached to any asset, such as a mortgage or margin loan, along with personal loans. Superannuation is also included as property, whether held in a normal fund or self- managed fund.

It is helpful if you can collect documents that show the value of your property, such as recent bank statements, property valuations or superannuation statements.

You may need to talk to a financial advisor or accountant about what you have, particularly if you're not sure. Sometimes one person in the relationship knows about all the financial information whereas the other person doesn't, and that's okay. Just pull together what you can.

You can refer to the property section in **Chapter 3** along with the **property checklist** in the **Resources** section of this book for more information and prompts about what type of property you might have to consider.

Think about what you want to achieve to resolve your matter before your appointment, and take time to write down any questions that you might have

While the outcome in your matter will likely be determined by applying the law relevant to your circumstances, it is still very important to consider your goals – the outcomes that you want to achieve in resolving your matter. These may change after you have received advice about outcomes, but setting goals prior to your first legal appointment will give you a clear direction where you are heading.

Think about the main questions you want to ask the lawyer. It is likely that you will have lots of questions and worries swirling around in your mind. Writing them down can help you focus on the important issues. A list of questions will also help your lawyer give you advice about those things that are concerning you, along with other advice you might need.

You can refer to the **questions and goals checklist** in the **Resources** section to help you formulate your own questions and goals.

Come with an open mind

You will likely come across friends and family who have had to deal with similar legal matters to yours, particularly in personal law matters such as family law. While it is important to be supported by friends and family through any dispute you might be facing, remember that your matter is different from anyone else's. Your family and circumstances surrounding your family are unique to you. There is no one-size-fits-all advice.

It may also be the case that your friends and family, as well-meaning as they might be, do not have all the information or legal knowledge to give you proper advice about your matter. It is not that you shouldn't listen to your friends and accept their support – simply be aware that unless they are lawyers practising in the field in which you are experiencing problems, the advice they give you might not be right for you.

Remember that your children are your priority

If you have children, they must remain your priority no matter what happens when you separate from your partner. With emotions running high and when you are in crisis mode, you will at some point focus on yourself. It is natural to do this. A relationship that you had with a person you love or once loved has ended, and you will feel a sense of loss. There will be times when you can think of nothing but getting through the pain you are suffering.

There will also be times when your partner is behaving badly and you want nothing more than to match their taunts and accusations. Don't. It's not worth it in the long run. Entering into the blame game or being drawn into tit-for-tat tactics will just wear you down and ultimately exhaust you. It is also not going to look great for you if your matter ends up before the court. And most importantly, regardless of how much you think you are shielding your children from it, your children are perceptive and will no doubt pick up on the conflict, however subtle.

As family lawyers, we know from social science research that the odds for children caught in the middle of parental conflict is not good. At best they will lose focus at school or generally be distracted; at worst they might suffer from serious mental health issues, drug addiction or have a higher risk of suicide.

By keeping your children at the front of your mind, you will ensure that your decisions and actions are based on providing them with the support they will need through this process. While it is difficult to take the high road and there will be occasions when you're just going to want to bite back, do all you can to resist it. You will be proud of yourself later when you manage to come through unscathed. Your children will make it through your separation never having seen the potential for ugliness that existed, and you will know that by taking the higher ground, there are no heat-of-the-moment things you could have said that can be used against you.

Look after yourself

Above all, look after yourself. It is one of the most stressful times you'll experience in your life. There is no detriment to you in seeking professional guidance, such as from a counsellor or psychologist, to help you through this. You might seek guidance to help you cope with the loss you are feeling from the end of your relationship, or to express in a safe space the anger you may be feeling. You might also find it helpful to seek advice on how to engage more constructively with the other parent in the particular circumstances of your separation.

If you have a mental illness, you should check in with medical professionals to help you. The end of your relationship is significant, and while you might think you are dealing with it okay, the stress and anxiety from resolving your situation, particularly your parenting situation, might trigger issues for you. It is best to seek help and be on the front foot so that you can continue to be there for your child or children.

Chapter 9:

Family law and empowered decision-making

Knowledge is power. Information is liberating. Education is the premise of progress, in every society, in every family.

— Kofi Annan

This is a popular proverb that you've probably come across before. In the context of family law matters, the application of the proverb might seem combative or litigious; however, when you consider the concept of empowered decision-making, 'knowledge is power' can be viewed in another way. Empowered decision-making as it applies to family law can be understood as the ability to determine your family law outcome having regard to the law, the system, your facts, the reality and your goals.

By having a good grasp on these variables, you can work towards resolving your matter and staying out of the family law system, or at least getting out of it as quickly as possible.

Having knowledge about the law, the system, your matter, the reality and how those variables align with your goals will give you the power to make decisions that accord with the outcomes you are trying to achieve. So yes, at its most basic level, knowledge is power. Having knowledge about your family law matter and the variables that apply liberates you to make the right decision for you. It is not a matter of being the most powerful, or having the right strategic move to outmanoeuvre the other party. It is about empowering you to make the right decision to resolve your dispute and move on with your life positively.

So what sort of knowledge are we talking about? I'm not suggesting that you need to enrol in a bachelor's degree or some short course in family law. It's not about going through four years of legal studies. It's certainly not about sitting down and reading the *Family Law Act* from cover to cover (and understanding it!).

The knowledge you need to empower yourself to make the best decisions for you is:

- a basic understanding of the law and the role of a lawyer as it applies to your matter;
- the best-case and worst-case scenarios for your matter; and
- how to make the most of the family law system.

WHAT DOES A FAMILY LAWYER DO?

Before embarking on any family law journey, I recommend investing in sensible, objective advice from a lawyer.

Getting advice early on is important. Even if you think you are on the right track, booking a consultation to see a family lawyer to discuss your proposal and receive some preliminary advice is vital. I regularly assist a number of clients with a preliminary strategy and advice session, and then hear from those clients that they have resolved their matter and now would like assistance with preparing the right documents.

In an initial consultation with a family lawyer, they will also be able to answer any concerns or doubts you have about what you can expect as part of your settlement. It is better to know these things up front than be heading off down the wrong path.

Regardless of where you are in your separation – considering taking the first step, having just separated or several months down the track – an initial consultation with a lawyer, perhaps even drafting a detailed strategy document, will at the very least put you on the right track to resolving your matter.

Take Kate, for example. Kate made an appointment with me for advice regarding her intention to end her de facto relationship. She believed that because the property they lived in was in her partner's name, she had no option but to walk away from the relationship empty-handed. They had been together for around six years and had a two-year-old child. As we talked through the options available to her, Kate became more confident in discovering that simply because the property was not in her name as well, or because she didn't make payments towards the mortgage, it did not mean that her contribution to the relationship was worthless; Kate had looked after the running of the household by cooking and cleaning and was primarily responsible for looking after their young child. The more we talked about the types of contributions in a relationship, the clearer it became there were options for Kate to reach a settlement that would involve an assessment of that contribution.

Had Kate not received that preliminary advice, she wouldn't have learned that there are many different types of contributions that are made and recognised in relationships.

Similarly, Tina met with me seeking some family law advice after becoming separated from the father of her two-year-old child. Tina was concerned at the prospect of the small child spending equal time with her and the father, but believed that it was the law and there was not much she could do about it. She had been worried about agreeing to something that just didn't feel right, but she felt that she had no option. After gaining legal advice about the *Family Law Act* and how the court might deal with parenting arrangements for a young child of two, Tina felt much more informed about the legal process and more confident moving forward in her negotiations with the father.

Tina then moved forward towards a mediation process with the right information about the law and a plan for the parenting arrangements for their child.

WHY DO YOU NEED A FAMILY LAWYER?

When the family law system is designed to allow you to represent yourself, you may ask, 'Why should I spend money on a lawyer?'

Courts recognise that not everyone can afford representation, because the reality is that lawyers cost money. For that reason you can absolutely go it alone through the family law system. Here are a few reasons why you might choose not to engage a lawyer after an initial consultation:

It's hard work!

Even as trained family lawyers, we find the work hard. It is an emotionally driven area of the law. Its primary purpose is to resolve disputes following the breakdown of relationships, which were no doubt entered into with hopes and dreams for a future full of love and shared respect.

If family law is hard work for the lawyer specialising in the area, how much harder would it be for the litigant attempting to traverse the system on their own?

Any family lawyer will tell you that if they found themselves in that scenario, there is no way they would put themselves through the family law system. It's a hard slog. Not only do you need to manage the legal aspects of your matter and convince the judge that your case is the preferred case based on the law and the evidence, but you need to prepare for your appearances, try to anticipate the outcomes, jump through all the legal hoops, follow the rules and the court orders, all while getting on and managing your day-to-day life, working, caring for your children, organising your children to get from A to B, somehow finding time to look after your emotional wellbeing, and trying to co-parent with your ex-spouse, who, a few days ago, was sitting at the other end of the bar table while the judge decided your interim parenting arrangements.

No, thank you. Give me a lawyer any day of the week to manage those things so I can get on with managing my life while we get through this process – that's what I would say. And why wouldn't you? A lawyer's training is specifically honed to help you manage these processes. They talk to judges in matters every day. They know what the rules are, and how to ensure that you comply with orders and the like. They allow you to get through the court appearance so you can get on with your everyday life without the added emotional and physical stress of managing your own matter.

Legal advice equals knowledge

This specialised knowledge provides you with the ability to make decisions tailored to your circumstances to get you off the family law merry-go-round and on with your life.

A lawyer will provide you with objective, realistic, strategic and commercial advice

Objective, realistic, strategic and commercial – it's a lot to cram in, but it's possible because of this one fact: while the lawyer can empathise with a client's circumstances and understand their predicaments, your children are not the lawyer's children and your property is not the lawyer's property. It sounds harsh, I know, but you wouldn't want it any other way. You need your lawyer to remain objective at all times; to tell you when to pull your head in; to save you from yourself. If not, you are wasting your money. If you can't get a straight answer from your lawyer or if you feel that your lawyer is just doing and saying things to make you feel better, rather than giving you objective advice, it's time to consider whether that lawyer is the right lawyer for you.

Realistic advice will make sure that your expectations are managed. There is little point in your lawyer telling you that you will achieve everything you are hoping for. Your lawyer must reality-test the outcomes you desire in line with the law and spell out the range of possible outcomes for your matter.

Your lawyer will provide you with strategic advice – how not to 'bid against yourself' at mediation; how to put your evidence before the court or in negotiations to ensure that your outcome aligns with your goals.

And lastly, your lawyer needs to provide you with commercial advice. A good lawyer will talk about making commercial decisions – how to resolve your matter, particularly property matters, in the most commercially advantageous manner.

A good lawyer will save you from yourself. If your family lawyer cannot approach your matter in this way, consider a second opinion.

Investing in this part of the process can be powerful. Armed with the lawyer's advice, you can then take the steps you need to take, either with or without a lawyer by your side. Remember that even in an instance where you do represent yourself, you may one day find yourself before a judge who will insist that you get some legal advice.

THE BEST-CASE AND WORST-CASE SCENARIOS FOR YOUR MATTER

Family lawyers talk in ranges. When you see a family lawyer for the first time, or after a couple of visits when all the information has been gathered, a family lawyer will give you a range into which your likely entitlement will fall, with several conditions attached. There is no certain outcome. Your family lawyer should not definitively inform you at your preliminary advice meeting that you will get x per cent of the property pool. If the lawyer does, consider whether you need a second opinion.

No family lawyer can, with any certainty, predict the likely outcome in your matter. The variables I discussed above will give you an indication about why that is the case. It is not because the lawyer is being cagey or because they want you to invest further time and money with them; it is because there is never any guaranteed outcome.

To work out your likely entitlement, your lawyer needs to consider your facts, the law, the evidence, how that evidence might be received by a court, your presentation, how you might go in the witness box, and the judge hearing your matter. Even considering all of these aspects, one judge might suggest the outcome lies between x and y, while the judge sitting in the next room might consider the outcome lies between y and z.

There are two other factors to consider. First, it is likely that your lawyer will tell you that the answer lies between x and y, while the lawyer representing your partner considers the answer to be between y and z. If you are faced with this scenario, don't despair. Remember that perceptions colour reality; how you see your contributions will more often than not be seen differently by your ex-partner.

The second factor, and probably the more important one, is to remember that you have a range of entitlement: from lowest to highest. Family lawyers find that clients tend to remember the highest percentage they will receive (within a quoted range) and the lowest amount it might cost them (again, within a quoted range). This is another important reason to have your preliminary advice provided to you in writing so that you can always refer back to the whole range and not just your best-case scenario.

You can take notes and write down key points, but remember it is also important to listen. You have invested your money in getting answers to your questions. Your lawyer may offer to provide written advice, but if they don't, you should ask for them to send you a short letter or email after the attendance summarising the key points. There may be an extra fee for this service depending on the lawyer you go to; however, it will be worth the investment, particularly where you find that when you get home, your mind goes blank and you can't remember some of the information and advice you received.

HOW TO MAKE THE MOST OF THE FAMILY LAW SYSTEM

So how do you navigate the family law system, the delays, the backlog? You focus on the alternatives. There are always alternative ways to resolve your dispute, such as taking advantage of compulsory mediation for your family law matter, or considering arbitration or collaborative models of resolving your dispute. These options were addressed in more detail in the previous chapters of this book.

Why take this approach to resolve your matter?

Why? The day you wake up knowing your future is certain, when your dispute has been resolved – that is why. The relief of knowing that you can get on with your life, look after your kids, work in your job without distraction, travel, enjoy life without stress … simply live. That's why. And why wouldn't you want to work towards that outcome?

HOW EMPOWERED DECISION-MAKING WILL ASSIST YOU

I have found in my years of legal practice that clients who readily resolve their matter are informed, goal-focused and understand the variables, including the reality. In my experience, I've found that by applying the following steps, clients are well on their way to resolve their matter through empowered decision-making:

1. Determine your goals.
2. Work out the reality of the personal legal issue to be resolved.
3. Source the knowledge as it applies to your matter.
4. Work out a tailored strategy to implement and work towards resolution.

Let's look at each of the steps a little more closely.

What are your goals?

Goals are important when dealing with your legal matter, particularly in family law. You need to consider what your goal is and how you will feel when you have achieved that goal. Quite often when speaking with clients about their family law issue, I find they haven't contemplated what their overall goal is – they know they are separating and that they are experiencing a state of flux, but they haven't turned their mind to what the end result might look like for them.

Some examples of goals might be:

- I would really like to retain the house if I can afford it.
- I'd like to keep the children at their private school as they only have three years to go.
- I really don't mind if my ex keeps the property – I'd be comfortable with enough cash to allow me to put a good deposit on a home.

When you go to see a lawyer for the first time about your matter, you should take the time to talk through what you would like to achieve.

You should listen to the advice about the law and the outcomes you can expect, and in this process consider whether your goals need refining. It is all well and good that your lawyer can tell you that you are entitled to x per cent of the whole property pool – but what does this mean for you? If x per cent means that you can't retain the house you want to retain or you are financially crippled carrying out terms, what is the point of the settlement?

Think about what your end game is and talk to your lawyer about how you can achieve this. It might be that those goals are less than your 'entitlement' at law.

Once you have settled on your goals, you should work through an action plan with your lawyer, setting out how to achieve the main goal and any smaller goals you set along the way.

If you approach your matter in this way, you will find that you are more focused in your endeavour to resolve your matter.

What is the reality of your personal legal issue?

It's important at the outset to work out what your personal legal issue is. You may think it is one thing, but working through the issue with your lawyer might lead you to realise it's something different to what you first thought. For example, many clients attend an initial advice session thinking they have to wait for 12 months before they can work out their parenting arrangements or property settlement. They've heard this from somewhere or someone. The reality is that the only thing they need to wait 12 months for is to lodge their application for divorce (see **Chapter 5**), which is different to arrangements for their children and property. These issues can usually be addressed straightaway.

This comes back to the individual nature of family law. It is important not to be disheartened by the reality. One of your lawyer's main jobs is to give you objective advice that challenges your reality. Without this objectivity you would expend a lot of money, several years of your life and all your emotional energy trying to achieve your expectations.

You need to have knowledge and understanding of the personalities involved in your matter. Only you will have this knowledge. You can describe the personalities of others involved in your matter to your lawyer and your lawyer will try to understand these personalities through their own perceptions; however, you are the only one who has lived your life dealing with these personalities every day. You alone will know the pressure points, what makes a person tick, what it will take to reach a decision – in the same way the other party to your dispute will know what makes you tick, how to press your buttons and the like.

Some examples here might be:

- You know that your ex-partner doesn't have a head for numbers, and so you suggest involving your accountant to sit down and talk through financial issues; or
- You know your ex-partner has a particular way of processing information and making decisions, so you ask your lawyer to communicate with your partner or their lawyer in a particular way.

Once you are clear on the issue to be resolved, you can start working towards how you might resolve it.

Source knowledge as it applies to your matter

It is important that you have a good understanding of the law as it applies to your matter, your best- and worst-case scenarios, an understanding of the variables that impact your matter, and how to work most efficiently through your matter.

You should ask your lawyer for detailed advice that you can understand and apply to your matter so that if your matter turns a particular direction you can understand why.

It may also help to note down the key points from that advice.

Which tailored strategy best suits your particular circumstances

Once you've worked out your goals and determined your legal issue to be resolved, and you have an understanding of the law as it applies to you, you need a strategy to resolve your matter.

Your lawyer should be able to assist you in creating a strategy document in the weeks that follow your initial appointment. There will be more information to gather and factors to consider; however, once all the information is to hand, an overall strategy that details the steps to take towards resolving your matter can be prepared and become the blueprint to work by.

A strategy document includes the goals you have discussed and the outcomes you hope to achieve. It will also include any specific tasks and timeframes, and who is responsible for attending to that task.

The emotional nature of many family law issues makes it all the more important to have an impartial person by your side. You will likely be feeling a range of emotions about your separation, and it is in your best interest not to let these emotions affect the way you proceed. For example, in considering property matters, if you are feeling guilty about the relationship ending, you may agree to a division that you later regret. It is important that you don't do anything to hurt your own chances of a reasonable settlement. Spending excessive amounts of money to remove it from the property pool, destroying property or lying about what property you own will likely result in deductions against you in the settlement.

There are also legal principles and rules that guide the division of joint property and it isn't always as simple as agreeing with your ex-spouse about who takes what. This is why it is a good idea to seek legal advice early on, to make sure you know your rights and entitlements. Even if you intend to divide the joint property yourself, by way of agreement, it is wise to speak to a lawyer initially so that you are aware of the kinds of issues that can arise and what your rights are.

A lawyer will also be able to draft the agreements between you both, and ensure this accurately and legally represents what you have agreed to. It is important for you to understand that if you divide your property by informal agreement between you and your former partner, they might later be able to make an action to get a further share from you. It is essential to make sure your property settlement is completed in a legally binding way, so that you are able to move forward without the possibility of further problems.

There may also be consequences for your tax obligations or insurance policies that you need to address. Your lawyer will be able to advise you on any such issues that arise, as well as the most beneficial approach to take in property divisions.

While separations can be messy and stressful, it is important that you look out for yourself by getting advice from someone who fully understands the law you are dealing with.

With a well-thought-out strategy you are well on your way to working towards achieving your goals, resolving your matter, and getting out of the family law system as soon as possible.

Throughout the whole process, regardless of which step you are up to, it is important to look after yourself. Let's now turn to the next chapter, where you'll find information and key tips to help you through your family law journey.

Chapter 10:

Looking after yourself

In this chapter you will find important information about looking after yourself during the family law process. It is important to follow some ground rules and reach out for counselling and financial support as you need it. There is absolutely no shame in admitting to yourself that you need some financial or emotional assistance to get through what is a very stressful process.

GROUND RULES FOR AN AMICABLE FAMILY LAW SETTLEMENT

You will have seen from what you have read so far that the family law process is significant and there are many positive reasons why you would work towards resolving your matter by the means set out in this book rather than going near the court system.

In order to give your negotiations the best chance of moving towards an amicable resolution, I'll share with you some tips based on what I've seen in my day-to-day practice as a family lawyer.

Understand that timing is everything

It is always a difficult time when a relationship or marriage ends, regardless of whether there are children or not. You will have built a relationship with a person and committed to spending your life with them. Often emotions run high. Sometimes logic fails. Regardless of how the end of your relationship came about, it is important to keep in mind the timing of when your relationship ended.

On occasions relationships end by mutual agreement. The parties decide that, for whatever reason, they no longer want to be in their relationship. More often, however, a relationship ends when one party decides that they no longer wish to be in the relationship. Often the person who decides to leave doesn't realise the impact that this decision has on the other partner. Because they have made their decision and have had the time to process that decision, they are at an advantage in dealing with the relationship breakdown.

It is important to remember that the other partner will be playing catch-up, particularly in the early part of any separation period. That person will be dealing with and making decisions potentially in a shell-shocked state, especially if the ending of the relationship caught them by surprise. This creates an imbalance in the positions of both parties at separation, and care must be taken to respect the circumstances relating to the separation.

If you ended the relationship, give your spouse ample time to heal and adjust to the separation. If you did not end the relationship, ask for time to heal and adjust to the separation. Don't push or be pushed into making quick decisions, particularly when there is an imbalance.

There are, of course, some advantages to a quick and easy settlement. If you are both on the same page, you have access to the same financial information and you know exactly what the circumstances are, you can negotiate a fast settlement to allow you both to move forward. However, those circumstances are the exception rather than the norm.

If settlements are rushed and financial information is missed or not disclosed, you potentially put your property settlement at risk. If your parenting matters are rushed, you might not be making decisions with a clear mind or thinking in the best interests of your children. Take the time to think through what you hope to achieve and make sure you have considered all possible outcomes without rushing.

Gather and share financial information

It is important to gather and share all financial information. It may be that one party possesses all the financial information while the other party knows very little about the financial circumstances of the relationship. In order for the parties to approach their negotiations fairly, it is important that both have access to information about their financial circumstances.

There is little point in hiding information soon after separation. This will only serve to backfire later, particularly where it leaves it open to the courts and the other party's solicitors making assessments under the *Family Law Act* to imply that documents have been hidden for a mischievous purpose. It is far better to approach any discussions about property and finances in a frank, open and honest manner.

Behave yourself

Your conduct at separation, and through any negotiations, will shape the nature of your family law negotiations and potentially affect their outcome. Be respectful of your spouse, particularly if they are the parent of your child or children. Do not engage in intimidating or harassing behaviour, or you may find yourself the subject of a protection order.

Separation is a hard enough process without also contending with bad behaviour. If you can maintain a sense of respect for the person you once held committed feelings for, you will come through your separation with a sense of dignity. If you feel that you are unable to do this, consider seeking guidance from a counsellor as you may be affected by feelings of grief, loss or even anger about the end of your relationship.

Do not air your grievances on social media

Facebook is not a private forum. While you might feel the urge to vent or rant about the frustrations you are enduring, permanently releasing those thoughts into the world of social media is not the solution. While Facebook is not evidence, it is often presented to the court either in the hope that it will prove a matter of some importance or paint a parent in a negative light – which is easily done when people are projecting their frustrations in an inappropriate forum without considering who the readers may be. In a court, where perception and presentation are important, when enough mud is thrown, some will inevitably stick.

Share the family photographs

If you have children, share the photographs of them with the other parent. Far too often I see a party determined to hurt the other by hanging onto family photographs and not allowing the other parent to have access to them. At one point in your relationship you both cared deeply enough about each other to have children. You need to put aside any feelings you may have about the other parent and allow them to at least share in the memories of the children you created together.

Writing things down will help you retain and resolve

The final tip in this section relates to the benefits of writing things down throughout your family law journey. Much is said of the benefits of journalling. I recall the compulsory requirement to keep a journal in my first year of high school – I wrote in it regularly, and I still have the journals in a box somewhere under our house. These days my journals are more like notebooks – a notebook for my book-planning, one for my work-planning, one for a particular committee, another for our life-planning. Lots of different notebooks for different purposes.

I have found that clients who take the time to make notes about the things they learn, questions they have and the answers they receive, are far better off than those who try to retain everything in their heads. By writing things down:

- You have a greater capacity to retain what you learn. You will work towards retaining the advice you receive about the law and the strategy to resolve your matter, which will in turn empower you to resolve your matter rather than thinking that you don't have the information you need to make the decision.

- You will gain the ability to think more broadly. Thinking and planning by using various mind-mapping tools on your computer has benefits, but the physical act of writing down your dreams, goals and business ideas on paper allows you to think more laterally. Noting down and tracking through your family law process in this manner will assist you to move forward towards resolution.

- Your thinking and planning becomes more focused. In today's technological world your computer is alive with notifications and distractions. At any given time you have email notifications, messages popping up, the constant feeding of the urge to check social media. Taking the time to write in a notepad gives you the opportunity to think and plan, free from distraction. It allows you to focus on what you are trying to plan, and to think more clearly. You can set out what issues you want to discuss with your family lawyer, any concerns you have, and how you anticipate you might work towards dealing with those concerns.

REMEMBER THAT IT'S OKAY TO ASK FOR HELP

Whether you need assistance in understanding financial arrangements or documents, or are not coping with your separation emotionally, there's no need to feel alone and unsupported. In addition to legal advice, it is important to also consider financial advice from a financial advisor or to seek out support for your mental wellbeing through attending sessions with a counsellor.

Counselling

Experiencing a separation is undeniably one of the most stressful events a person can go through in their lifetime, ranking alongside the death of a loved one and purchasing a home. The spectrum of emotions that may be encountered during this process can be overwhelming, and even the simplest of separations can trigger intense feelings of anxiety. Prior to the separation, you may have been a well-adjusted and confident individual, but in the aftermath may find yourself unrecognisable, plagued with feelings of despair and a range of extreme emotions. It is common to feel emotionally fragile, lethargic and irritable, which affects your interactions with friends and family. However, it is important to remember that this is only temporary and seeking support can help you navigate through this confronting time.

Separation can be a challenging and emotional time for the individuals involved. The loss of a partner and the end of a relationship can bring about a sense of grief and mourning for a future that once seemed certain. There may also be feelings of guilt or shame, sadness, anger, confusion and fear. The loss of a shared future and the dissolution of a partnership can cause feelings of betrayal, rejection and loneliness, and it can take time for each partner to navigate through these stages. In addition to these emotional responses, individuals may also feel overwhelmed by the practical considerations of separating, such as dividing assets, finding a new place to live and adjusting to a new routine.

It is essential for both partners to give themselves time to mourn the end of their partnership and seek support from friends, family or a therapist. It is also crucial for both partners to communicate openly and honestly about their feelings and needs to move forward in a healthy and respectful manner.

shock.

anger.

guilt.

barga
ining.

depre
ssion.

accep
tance.

time.

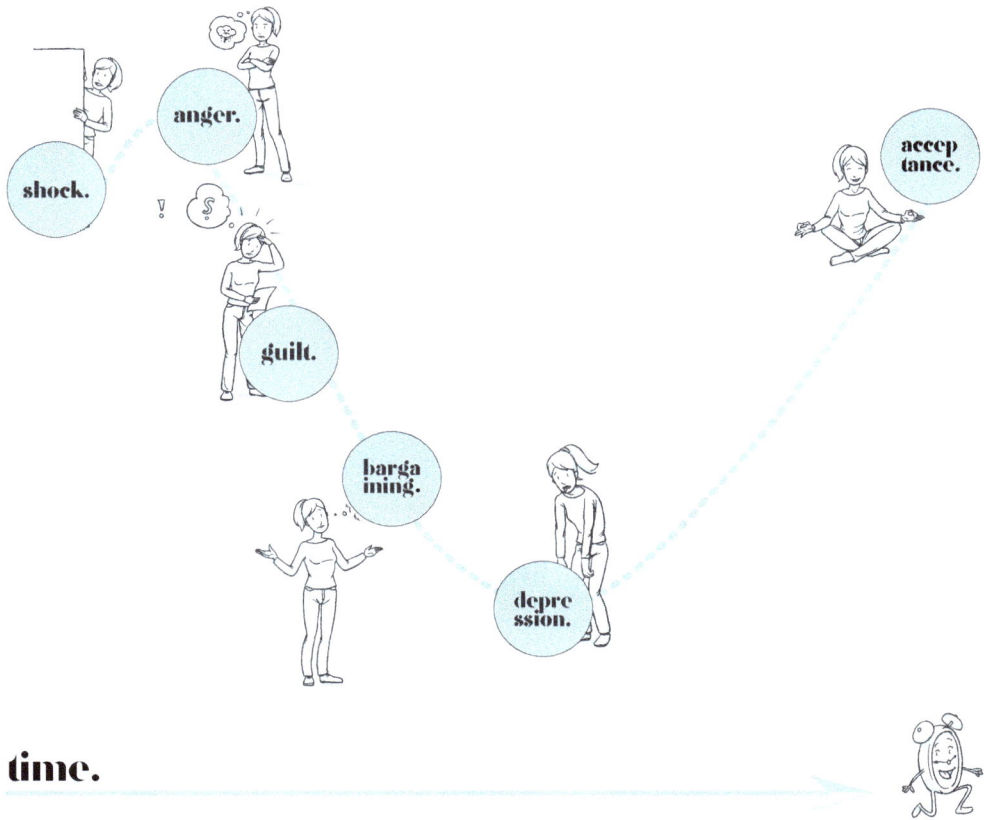

Making your mental health a priority is essential as it impacts your ability to navigate through negotiations and, most importantly, care for any children. As with the loss of a loved one, the stages of grief are also experienced during separation and can include emotions such as denial, anger, bargaining, depression and acceptance. It's important to recognise that everyone's journey is unique, and there's no 'right' way to grieve. However, prioritising your mental health and seeking support when you need it can help you move through the stages of grief and emerge stronger on the other side.

Emma had been married to her husband for ten years. The couple had grown apart over the years, and Emma found herself feeling lonely and disconnected in the partnership. After initial separation, Emma felt a mix of emotions ranging from sadness and grief to fear and uncertainty. She struggled to come to terms with the end of her marriage and felt overwhelmed by the many practical and emotional challenges that came with separation. However, with the help of a counsellor and the support of her loved ones, Emma was able to work through her feelings and develop a plan for moving forward.

Reaching out to trusted friends, family members or a professional counsellor can help you navigate the challenges and emotions of the separation process. Simply having someone to listen and provide reassurance that you're on the right track can be incredibly helpful in reducing feelings of anxiety and uncertainty. Remember, you don't have to go through this alone, and seeking support is a powerful and positive step towards healing and moving forward.

How can a counsellor assist you during separation?
Counsellors can provide valuable support to individuals experiencing a separation by offering a safe and confidential space for them to explore and process their thoughts and feelings, identify patterns of behaviour that may be contributing to the separation, and develop strategies for coping with the changes and challenges that arise during this time. Additionally, a counsellor can facilitate healthy communication between partners, which can be especially beneficial when there are children involved.

Counselling can help individuals build resilience and develop a positive outlook for the future. A counsellor may also provide referrals to other professionals, such as solicitors or financial advisors, to help individuals navigate the practical aspects of separation.

Reaching out for help is not a sign of weakness, in fact it is a proactive and positive response to a difficult situation and allows you to develop coping skills and explore practical strategies to navigate what is an intense and difficult time. It creates a safe space to allow the grief and sense of loss to be appropriately explored and the opportunity to begin to rebuild, and plan for what your 'new normal' is going to look like, empowering individuals to move forward with their lives and thrive after the separation.

Counsellors can also play a vital role in supporting communication with children. Separation can have a significant impact on children, and it's important to handle the situation in a way that promotes their wellbeing and minimises the potential for long-term negative effects. With the help of a counsellor, individuals can gain insight into their children's perspectives and emotions, as well as learn effective communication strategies to help their children understand and cope with the separation.

A mental health professional offered five tips to assist individuals experiencing a separation from a wellbeing perspective:

1. *Allow yourself the gift of time.* Don't rush the process or panic. Take the time to be kind to yourself, even as you experience the pain of loss. Surround yourself with people and things you love to remind yourself that life remains rich and good, despite your current situation.

2. *Seek support.* Ending a significant relationship like a marriage or domestic partnership is a significant life event. Don't underestimate the impact this can have on your wellbeing. Invest in yourself and seek the help of a counsellor to debrief what you've been through and consider how you can grow through this experience.

3. *Prioritise self-care.* Even if you feel terrible, try not to act on those negative feelings. Focus on cultivating healthy habits such as eating well, getting enough sleep, exercising and doing things you enjoy. Nutrition, daily activity, rest and the company of supportive friends are essential components of wellbeing at any stage of life, but especially important during a time of loss. Taking care of yourself can help you heal and grow stronger.

4. *Focus on the present.* Try not to dwell on the past or worry too much about the future. Instead, focus on the present moment and take things one day at a time.

5. *Find ways to relieve stress.* Engage in activities that help you relax and reduce stress, such as practising mindfulness, yoga or meditation. It's important to take breaks from the stress of the separation and find ways to centre yourself.

Remember, separation can be a difficult and emotional process, but by prioritising your wellbeing and seeking support, you can navigate it with greater ease and emerge stronger on the other side.

Financial advice

You should also talk to a financial advisor or accountant, particularly if you are not sure what property you have or if you aren't quite sure how to deal with any property that you receive.

Generally, when you separate you are very much in survival mode. Quite often you are just going through the motions to do what you can to get through each day. This survival mode comes from circumstances where everything has been going along okay and then all of a sudden your life is turned upside down and you need to make lots of decisions quickly – and most of them involve money. You might go from a two-income household to a one- or no-income household. You are trying to work out how you are going to feed the children, keep the power on, where you are going to live.

It is important at that point to take a step back from worrying so much about what the future finances might look like, and instead ask yourself the question of how you're going to survive financially between now and when a settlement might happen. What is required today for you to keep the lights on?

Gino Saggiomo from Rothgard Financial Services says that if you don't seek financial advice and aren't clear on what your base position is (what it takes to keep the lights on), you will continue to make financial decisions based on emotions and what you believe is fair and equitable.

Gino gives the example of a client (let's call her Lucy) who threw her hands up and effectively said to her ex-partner, 'It's all too hard. I can't be bothered. Just give me whatever you want.' Gino explains that Lucy had been used to working part-time for the last 15 years and had three children. Immediately after separation, Lucy purchased a property with only a 10% deposit with very high repayments. She had never rented in her life, so she thought that ownership of property would be the only way to move forward, even though renting in the short term would have been much easier on the weekly budget. In addition, on settlement Lucy received a couple of hundred thousand dollars but, rather than planning wisely and paying money into her mortgage, she went on a financial 'bender' spending everything she received, with the net result that her part-time wage wasn't enough to support her financial lifestyle.

Gino's role in that situation was to counsel Lucy to relinquish the property that she owned because financially she couldn't hang onto it. Gino reflects that it was quite sad for Lucy – it was a mess that all came down to her making an emotional, rash decision to get her ex-partner 'out of her life'.

How can a financial advisor assist you during separation?

A financial advisor can provide a voice of reason in a stressful and chaotic stage of your life. Over the years of dealing with clients, I've found that in relationships, either both partners know everything about the ins and outs of the finances or, more often, one person has managed the finances and the other has little or no idea about the details. For the person who knows nothing about the finances, the financial aspect of separation can be quite scary.

A good financial advisor – that is, one who is appropriately qualified and has the necessary specialised accreditation – will have an ability to provide a sense of calm, much like one of the key qualities of your family lawyer. At the outset they will quickly be able to assist you in working through your income and expenditure – what money is coming in and what it takes to keep the lights on.

Gino has three tips to help you from a financial wellbeing perspective:

- Probably the most important one: understand that big decisions don't have to be made now. Gino says he always uses the example of Lucy with people who are going through separation – just because you've never rented before in your life doesn't mean you need to buy a house while you're in the middle of a separation.
- Understand the bottom line: what is the minimum you need from a settlement to be okay, and that will maintain equilibrium for you?
- Understand your budget: what does it take to keep your personal finances running every year and understanding where and what your financial war chest is? That is, if you don't have a lot of money saved up, is there a way you can access some capital relatively quickly, particularly if you need to fund your lifestyle and expenses while you're going through your family law matter?

It's important to understand that separation is generally an unstable and unpredictable time. There are going to be expenses that come up out of nowhere. You might find out information about your ex-partner that totally blindsides you. Your ex-partner may start behaving badly and the kids might become difficult. There are so many different variables. What is important in all of this is to hang onto the knowledge that everything will work out eventually, in some form or another. It will end and you will be okay.

Conclusion

When I set out to write this book, I wanted to provide a manual of sorts for people contemplating or experiencing separation. It is very much a guide only; as I have said throughout, it is important that you seek legal advice relevant to your own personal needs.

As you will have seen from the pages within this book, the family law system is complex, full of many different and competing variables. The court process is long and at times costly. You may be making decisions in crisis mode, having just been told your relationship is over. You are all of a sudden trying to get by on one income or no income at all. All the while, you have the task of ensuring that your children are insulated from any conflict or uncertainty about their living arrangements.

It is important to remember that in the midst of all this chaos, there is light at the end of the tunnel. You will come out of your family law process, you will put your life back together, and you will move onwards and upwards to bigger and better things.

To achieve this outcome in the best way possible, I recommend taking on board the information I've provided in this book, particularly in **Chapters 8, 9 and 10**. The process you follow to get yourself through your separation – avoiding court if at all possible, and if not, getting out of court as soon as you can – will only allow you to move on to a new life sooner.

Taking the time to listen to the advice your family lawyer gives you and trying to understand the law and its processes as much as you can will mean that you are more empowered to make informed decisions and resolve your matter.

Bibliography

Over my years of study and practice, I have referred to many textbooks and guides. My learning and knowledge are shaped further by things I read every day. Those books and references that have guided me and helped me to distil key concepts are set out below:

STATISTICS

Marriages and Divorces, Australia, 2021, released 11 November 2022. Most recently accessed 17 June 2023.
https://www.abs.gov.au/statistics/people/people-and-communities/marriages-and-divorces-australia/latest-release

Federal Circuit and Family Court of Australia, 2021-22 Annual Report. Most recently accessed 17 June 2023 https://www.fcfcoa.gov.au/fcfcoa-annual-reports/2021-22

Family Court of Western Australia, Annual Review 2022. Most recently accessed 17 June 2023. https://www.familycourt.wa.gov.au/_files/Publications_Reports/Annual_Review_2022.pdf

LEGISLATION & CASE LAW (AVAILABLE AT WWW.AUSTLII.EDU.AU)

Family Law Act 1975 (Cth) (as amended).
Marriage Act 1961 (Cth).
Domestic and Family Violence Protection Act 2012 (Qld).

The four-step exercise referred to on page 35 comes from the case of *Hickey and Hickey and the Attorney General for the Commonwealth of Australia (Intervenor)* (2003) 30 Fam LR 355.

COURT PRACTICE DIRECTIONS

The Family Law Case Management Central Practice Direction issued by the Federal Circuit and Family Court of Australia. Most recently accessed 17 June 2023.

https://www.fcfcoa.gov.au/fl/pd/fam-cpd

BOOKS AND OTHER REFERENCE MATERIAL

Family Law Book (available by subscription at www.thefamilylawbook.com.au)

Australian Master Family Law Guide (published by Wolters Kluwer, CCH Australia Limited, Sydney) with the 11th edition published in

December 2021 and the 12th edition due in November 2023 (https://shop.wolterskluwer.com.au/items/10076409-0007S, accessed 17 June 2023).

Family Law Principles – Alexandra Harland, Donna Cooper, Zoe Rathus, Renata Alexander with contributing editor Chris Turnbull, Third Edition, Law Book Co, 2021

Family Law – Anthony Dickey QC, Fifth Edition, Law Book Co, 2007

Collaborative Divorce – Pauline Tesler, William Morrow Paperbacks; Reprint edition (12 June 2007)

Lizette Borreli, 'Why Using Pen And Paper, Not Laptops, Boosts Memory: Writing Notes Helps Recall Concepts, Ability To Understand' 6 February 2014 http://www.medicaldaily.com/why-using-pen-and-paper-not-laptops-boosts-memory-writing-notes-helps-recall-concepts-ability-268770 (accessed 17 June 2023)

Acknowledgements

Writing this book was a huge learning process for me. Write a book, they said. It will be easy, they said. I started a program and had the best mentors and advice around. It was great, I was all in and working through the necessary steps to write a book – to share all the knowledge in my head with you.

One weekend I had a particularly successful writing session. I sat with my headphones on, fingers typing away. I clocked up 12,000 words in less than 48 hours. Woohoo – what an achievement! I was nearly halfway there!

What I didn't realise was that the intense amount of pressure that I put myself under, along with an overwhelming amount of ongoing stressors in work and life, can trigger severe eye strain. It did in my case – so much so that I then had to embark on about four months of intensive steroid-based treatment for my right eye, up to 12 drops per day every day. You could say I became typing-shy for a long time. I felt completely unable to achieve what I'd set out to achieve. I was overly conscious of avoiding the computer screen. I had been told that if the drops didn't work, I would be facing a steroid injection into my eye. As a person with a deep fear of injections, that idea was frightening.

At the same time, work started to overwhelm me. I felt there were days when I couldn't do my job, days when I didn't want to do my job. I even started to question whether I wanted to be a lawyer at all anymore. It was a difficult period, and it took some good advice, patience, time and more learning to get through it.

So what did I take away from this turbulent time?

- That every day is indeed a school day – we learn more and more about how we can and can't do things, what our limits are, what the best process is for dealing with any given thing.
- I know that if I don't have time out to spend on myself, my body, mind and soul, it is really hard to keep doing what I love doing.
- I learned that I am curious by nature – I guess I've always known that, but it's nice to have something of a label for things like my love of big aeroplanes and how they stay in the air.
- That I do love being a lawyer, and the very core of that is a deep and embedded love of learning and knowledge, and an ability to impart that knowledge on others.

So I pressed on, and now you are reading the finished product. I was consciously blinking more than I might ordinarily. I was focused and I have found that I am now even more passionate about what I do.

I owe some personal thankyous:

- To **my clients,** who took the time to give me crucial feedback. Your stories are what make me keep doing what I do. Thank you.

- To **Marcia** for your original guidance (you are missed) and to my social work colleagues and to **Gino** – your guidance has shaped how I have assisted my clients through the years. Your input was invaluable to me. Thank you.

- To my close mentors and friends, whose passion for family law and alternative dispute resolution is unwavering, whose knowledge, experience and personalities have influenced my practice as a family lawyer and whose friendship and mentorship have been invaluable to me throughout this journey.

- To my original assistant researchers **Phoebe** and **Luke**, thank you. The additional research you did helped me to pull all this together without overwhelming myself!

- To **Helen**, for your support and for transcribing long interviews.

- To **my amazing team, past and present, at Life Law Solutions**, who rode this wave with me and kept everything ticking along, particularly on writing days!

- To my friends **Rachel, Jenny** and **Ann**, who kept picking me up when I lost momentum and prodding me to get this done.

- To **my family** for their support, particularly to my mum, **Sue**, who handed on to me her love of lifelong learning. I am what I am today because of you. Thank you.

- And to **my husband Fraser**. I couldn't have achieved all that I have achieved without you standing beside me, picking me up and keeping me going. Your love and support for me means so much.

Resources

AUTHOR CONTACT DETAILS

Elizabeth Fairon is a Legal Practice Director at Life Law Solutions. You can contact Elizabeth at either her Brisbane or Sunshine Coast office as follows:

P: 07 3343 9522 or 07 5446 1745

Email: mail@lifelaw.com.au

Web: www.lifelaw.com.au

LinkedIn: @elizabethfairon

DE FACTO RELATIONSHIP RESOURCES

Registering a civil partnership

Queensland	https://www.qld.gov.au/law/ births-deaths-marriages-and-divorces/marriage-weddings-and-civil-partnerships/civil-partnerships/ registering-a-civil-partnership

New South Wales	http://www.bdm.nsw.go http://www.bdm.nsw.gov.au/v.au/Pages/apply-for-certificates/apply-for-certificates.aspxrelationship
Victoria	https://www.bdm.vic.gov.au/marriages-and-relationships/register-a-domestic-relationship
Australian Capital Territory	https://www.accesscanberra.act.gov.au/app/answers/detail/a_id/1694!tabs-1
Tasmania	http://www.justice.tas.gov.au/bdm/relationships/register
South Australia	https://www.sa.gov.au/topics/family-and-community/births,-deaths-and-marriages/register-a-relationship
Northern Territory	Northern Territory is one of two jurisdictions in Australia (the other being Western Australia) not to offer relationship registries and official domestic partnership schemes.
Western Australia	Western Australia is one of two jurisdictions in Australia (the other being the Northern Territory) not to offer relationship registries and official domestic partnership schemes.

Ending a civil partnership

Queensland	https://www.qld.gov.au/law/births-deaths-marriages-and-divorces/marriage-weddings-and-civil-partnerships/civil-partnerships/end-a-civil-partnership
New South Wales	http://www.bdm.nsw.gov.au/Pages/apply-for-certificates/apply-for-certificates.aspxrelationship

Victoria	https://www.bdm.vic.gov.au/ marriages-and-relationships/revoke-a-relationship
Australian Capital Territory	There is a link to download an application form in the FAQ section – https://www.accesscanberra.act. gov.au/app/answers/detail/a_id/1694!tabs-2
South Australia	https://www.sa.gov.au/topics/family-and-community/births,-deaths-and-marriages/ register-a-relationship/de-register-a-relationship

REGISTRIES OF BIRTHS, DEATHS & MARRIAGES

Queensland	https://www.qld.gov.au/law/ births-deaths-marriages-and-divorces Address: Level 32, 180 Ann Street, Brisbane Qld 4001 Phone: 13 QGOV (13 74 68)
New South Wales	http://www.bdm.nsw.gov.au/ Address: GPO Box 30, Sydney NSW 2001 Phone: 13 77 88
Victoria	https://www.bdm.vic.gov.au/ Address: GPO Box 4332, Melbourne Vic. 3001 Phone: 1300 369 367
Australian Capital Territory	https://www.accesscanberra.act.gov. au/app/answers/detail/a_id/18/~/ apply-for-a-birth%2C-death-or-marriage-certificate Address: GPO Box 158, Canberra ACT 2601 Phone: 13 22 81
Tasmania	http://www.justice.tas.gov.au/bdm Address: 30 Gordons Hill Road, Rosny Park Tas. 7018 Phone: 1300 135 513

South Australia	https://www.sa.gov.au/topics/ family-and-community/ births,-deaths-and-marriages Address: GPO Box 1351, Adelaide SA 5001 Phone: 131 882
Northern Territory	https://nt.gov.au/law/bdm Address: GPO Box 3021, Darwin NT 0801 Phone: (08) 8999 6119
Western Australia	http://www.bdm.dotag.wa.gov.au/ Address: PO Box 7720, Cloisters Square, Perth WA 6850 Phone: 1300 305 021

OTHER KEY FAMILY LAW AGENCIES

Relationships Australia: https://www.relationships.org.au/1300 364 277

Family Relationships: http://www.familyrelationships.gov.au/ Pages/default.aspx1800 050 321

Services page: http://www.familyrelationships.gov.au/Services/ Pages/default.aspx

Centacare: http://centacarebrisbane.net.au/Phone: 1300 236 822

Anglicare: https://anglicaresq.org.au/children-and-families/family-and-relationship-support/relationship-support/Phone: 1300 610 610

Better Relationships: http://betterrelationships.org.au/services/ counselling/Phone: 1300 114 397

Family & Relationship Services Australia Directory: https:// frsa.org.au/our-members Lists centres all throughout Australia.

Legal Aid Queensland: http://www.legalaid.qld.gov.au/Find-legal-information/Relationships-and-children**1300 651 188**

DOMESTIC AND FAMILY VIOLENCE RESOURCES

Domestic violence legislation and support services:

Queensland	Domestic and Family Violence Protection Act 2012 DV Connect **1800 811 811**
New South Wales	Crimes (Domestic and Personal Violence) Act 2007 Domestic Violence Line **1800 65 64 63**
Victoria	Family Violence Protection Act 2008; Family Violence Reform Implementation Monitor Act 2016 Safe Steps Family Violence Response Centre **1800 015 188 or (03) 9322 3555**
Australian Capital Territory	Domestic Violence and Protection Orders Act 2008 *Domestic Violence Crisis Service* **(02) 6280 0900**
Tasmania	Family Violence Act 2004 Family Violence Response Referral Line **1800 633 937**
South Australia	Domestic Violence Act 1994 Domestic Violence Crisis Service 1300 782 200 Domestic Violence and Aboriginal Family Violence Gateway Service **1800 800 098**
Northern Territory	Domestic and Family Violence Act 2007 Dawn House **(08) 8945 1388**

Western Australia	Restraining Orders Act 1997 Women's Domestic Violence Helpline: **1800 007 339** or **(08) 9223 1188**

The online domestic violence application forms can be located here:

Queensland	http://www.courts.qld.gov.au/__data/assets/ pdf_file/0006/162168/dva-f-1.pdf
South Australia	http://www.courts.sa.gov.au/Lists/Forms/ Attachments/1323/Form%2028AA%20-%20 Private%20Application.pdf
Tasmania	http://www.magistratescourt.tas.gov.au/ going_to_court/restraint_orders
Western Australia	http://www.magistratescourt.wa.gov.au/r/ restraining_orders.aspx
Northern Territory	https://nt.gov.au/law/courts-and- tribunals/domestic-violence-orders/ how-to-apply-for-a-domestic-violence-order

Other domestic violence support services across Australia:

The National Sexual Assault, Family & Domestic Violence
    Counselling Line: **1800 737 732**
Lifeline: **13 11 14**
Translating & Interpreting Service: **131 450**
Suicide Call Back Service: **1300 659 467**
Mensline Australia: **1300 789 978**
Kids Help Line: **1800 551 800**
Australian Childhood Foundation: **1800 176 453**
Relationships Australia: **1300 364 277**

Penda App: Penda is a free app with legal, financial and personal safety information and referrals for women who have experienced domestic and family violence. Download from the App Store.

CHILD SUPPORT RESOURCES

Limited Child Support Agreement: https://www.humanservices.gov. au/sites/default/files/2017/08/cs1666-1706en.pdf

CHECKLISTS

On the following pages you will find:

- property checklist
- questions and goals checklist

These are also available for download at www.lifelaw.com.au

★ All websites and links current at 6 July 2023 ★

Your Property Checklist

life law

SOLUTIONS

YOUR PROPERTY CHECKLIST

☐ Date you started living together:

☐ Date you got married:

☐ Date you separated:

Thinking back...

When you started living together, **what did you own?**
Use a description if you can

What did you own?	Estimated Value
House	
Unit / Townhouse	
Car #1	
Car #2	
Shares / Investments	
Other Investments	
Interests in a Company	
Interests in a Trust	
Money in the bank	

When you started living together, **what did you owe?**

What did you own?   **Estimated Value**

    Mortgage

    Other loans

    Credit card

    Car loan

When you started living together, **what superannuation did you have?**

Fund name: **Estimated Value**

Thinking back...

When you started living together, **what did you spouse own?**
Use a description if you can

What did they own?	Estimated Value
House	
Unit / Townhouse	
Car #1	
Car #2	
Shares / Investments	
Other Investments	
Interests in a Company	
Interests in a Trust	
Money in the bank	

When you started living together, **what did your spouse owe?**
Use a description if you can

What did they owe?	Estimated Value
Mortgage	
Other loans	
Credit card	
Car loan	

When you started living together, **what superannuation did they have?**

Fund name: **Estimated Value**

Make some notes...

What was your working history during your relationship? What roles did you have? What was your average salary?

What about your spouse? What was their working history, roles and average salary?

Did either of your parents or other family members give you money during your relationship? Or contribute to buying property for you?

Did you have any other significant cash monies come into your family during your relationship? From injury claims, inheritances, winning the lotto?

Thinking about now...

What property do you now have together whether it is in your name,
your spouses name or joint names.
Use a description if you can

What do you own?	Estimated Value
House	
Unit / Townhouse	
Car #1	
Car #2	
Shares / Investments	
Other Investments	
Interests in a Company	
Interests in a Trust	
Money in the bank	

What do you owe?	Estimated Value
Mortgage	
Other loans	
Credit card	
Car loan	

Questions and goals checklist.

life law
SOLUTIONS

QUESTIONS & GOALS
CHECKLIST

What are the **top three goals** for your parenting matter?

Why are these goals so important for you?

How will you feel when you achieve these goals?

What are the **top three goals** for your property matter?

Why are these goals so important for you?

How will you feel when you achieve these goals?

www.ingramcontent.com/pod-product-compliance
Lightning Source LLC
Chambersburg PA
CBHW040853210326
41597CB00029B/4823